Cleavage Shift in Colombia:
Analysis of the 1970 Elections

JUDITH TALBOT CAMPOS

Division of Social Sciences and Economics
Universidad del Valle

JOHN F. McCAMANT

Graduate School of International Studies
University of Denver

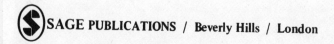

SAGE PUBLICATIONS / Beverly Hills / London

For information address:

SAGE PUBLICATIONS, INC.
275 South Beverly Drive
Beverly Hills, California 90212

SAGE PUBLICATIONS LTD
St George's House / 44 Hatton Garden
London E C 1

International Standard Book Number 0-8039-0176-3

Library of Congress Catalog Card No. 72-84040

FIRST PRINTING

CONTENTS

LIST OF TABLES AND FIGURES

Cleavage Shift in Colombia:
Analysis of the 1970 Elections

JUDITH TALBOT CAMPOS
Universidad del Valle

JOHN F. McCAMANT
University of Denver

On April 19, 1970, Colombian citizens went to the polls to give their verdict in the most hotly contested presidential election since 1946. The selection of the president by the two parties participating in the National Front government had received a major challenge from ex-dictator Gustavo Rojas Pinilla and his movement, *Alianza Nacional Popular* (Anapo). After the initial returns showed Rojas ahead, he claimed the victory and refused to recognize the later returns that gave Misael Pastrana the lead. The final official returns gave the victory to Pastrana by 53,000 votes: Misael Pastrana Borrera, 1,614,419 (40.6%); Gustavo Rojas Pinilla, 1,561,468 (39.2%); Belisario Betancur, 470,445 (11.8%); Evaristo Sourdis, 335,286 (8.4%). The two-party system of Liberals and Conservatives, which had existed for 120 years had come to an end. Third parties had risen and fallen, usually being incorporated into the traditional parties, but none had ever before been able to capture sufficient popular support to

AUTHORS' NOTE: *The authors are grateful to the many persons in Cali and Denver who helped in the research for this monograph. John C. Hammock helped organize the field research; Jose Vicente Katarain acted as research assistant in Cali; Dr. Gustavo Arango Veliz provided many useful contacts with members of Anapo; Glenn Newkirk helped with the computer work in Denver; Ken Switzer gave useful suggestions for change on the finished monograph; Sally McCamant and German Campos gave the kind of support that only spouses can give; the Rockefeller Foundation financed the field research and travel to and from Colombia. The deficiences that remain are our responsibility.*

become a contender with the major parties. The challenge of Anapo was more threatening to the political elite of Colombia because Anapo received most of its support from the lower class. Almost none of the upper class voted for it. The traditional cleavage based on weakening clerical/anti-clerical differences was, at least in 1970, replaced by a cleavage based on class.

At the time of the 1970 elections, Anapo was not yet a third party. Under the regulations of the National Front agreement, all presidential candidates in 1970 had to come from the Conservative Party, the Liberals having had the presidency in the 1966-1970 period. General Rojas, then, ran as a Conservative candidate, and all the Anapo candidates for representative offices ran on either Conservative Anapo or Liberal Anapo lists. Anapo formally declared itself a party in June 1971. Thus, the 1970 election provided an ambiguous test for Anapo as a "third party." With the aging of General Rojas and his leaving the leadership of the movement to this daughter, Maria Eugenia Rojas de Moreno Diaz, and the renewal of party competition in the presidential elections of 1974, a more definitive test will come soon. It is not yet certain that the traditional two-party system will be superseded permanently by a new system, either a three-party or a multiparty system, or a different two-party system with a strong class basis.

The vote in 1970 in Colombia demonstrated a class cleavage of greater strength than seems to exist anywhere else in Latin America today and compares with the strongest class cleavages in Europe. In Colombia, 60 to 65% of the lower class, which makes up about two-thirds of the urban population, voted for Anapo. In Scandanavia and Italy, where the working-class makes up only about half of the population, the lower-class party or parties received about 70% of the working-class vote (Rose and Urwin, 1969). Anapo, unlike the European parties, does not preach class divisions or class struggle, but only asks that the lower classes receive more benefits. It is a populist party rather than a marxist party, but it has had greater class appeal than has usually been the case among populist parties.

Only two Latin American countries, Argentina and Chile, presently have political parties organized along class lines to any extent. We do not have comparable information on voting in those two countries, but the data available indicate that the class split is somewhat less than it was in the 1970 elections in Colombia. In the 1962 elections in Argentina, the last in which the Peronists were able to present candidates, the Peronist vote in three working-class districtis was 35.5, 44.0, and 52.7% of the total (Rowe, n.d.: 32-33). In Chile, the vote for Salvador Allende in 1958 and 1964 in working-class districts did not surpass 44% in the cities and reached only 51% in the isolated mining regions (Gil and Parrish, 1965: 47).

The sudden rise of a new party based on lower-class support to the point where it obtained 40% of the national vote is very rare in world history. When similar shifts occurred in Europe, they came with the extension of suffrage, but Colombia has had universal male suffrage since 1910. Furthermore, a smaller percentage of the electorate is presently voting than was the case 10 or even 25 years ago. The Colombian case required more than the building of new loyalties; it required the destruction of old loyalties to the traditional parties, which only exceptional circumstances could bring about. The object of this monograph is to probe the historical and behavioral characteristics of this cleavage shift in order to explain how and why it happened.

The basis for this shift is rooted in the historical events of the last 25 years, but knowledge of these events did not allow anyone, and certainly not the authors, to predict the 1970 elections. The absence of public knowledge about the attitudes of the Colombian electorate and the activities of the Anapo movement meant that the results of the 1970 election came as a surprise to nearly all observers. An understanding of the 1970 election, then, required the gathering of new information. The Division of Social Sciences and Economics of the Universidad del Valle decided to analyze the views of the electorate, first in a small way in 1968 and then with a larger effort in 1970. One of us (Campos) organized a survey of over 2,000 rural, town, and city residents in the Department of Valle de Cauca before the 1970 elections and followed up after the elections with a survey of over 1,000 residents of the city of Cali (see appendix for details). The surveys provide representative information for one department of Colombia, but this department shares socioeconomic and political characteristics with the other two more developed departments of Antioquia and Cundinamarca. Together, these three departments provided nearly half the national votes. National election statistics and a survey conducted by the Department of Political Science of the Universidad de los Andes in Bogota provided confirmation for our general conclusions based on the surveys in the Department of Valle de Cauca.

The information provided by the surveys and the election results of 1970 provide a new perspective for looking at historical events in Colombia. We begin with the development of and changes in the traditional party cleavage and continue with the undermining of the popular base of the traditional parties by the removal of interparty competition in the National Front, the weak policy reforms of the Front, and the poor economic conditions. Anapo, whose original purpose seemed simply to vindicate the name and reputation of General Rojas, took full advantage of the opportunity provided by this political and economic situation. After discussion of this background, we go into the analysis of the campaign and the election. In the end, we bring the analysis up to date with a brief discussion of events since the 1970 election.

THE TRADITIONAL PARTY CLEAVAGE

Colombia and Uruguay are the only Latin American countries with regularly contested elections which preserved the traditional two-party system predominant throughout Latin America in the nineteenth century. In other countries, the "liberal" and "conservative" parties have either died out entirely or have failed to maintain support among the popular classes, which have turned toward socialist, "revolutionary," Christian democratic, or populist parties. In Colombia, as in Uruguay, the loyalties to the two traditional parties existed among all classes with an intensity that persisted through the generations.

The Conservative-Liberal cleavage in Colombia was first clearly drawn in 1848, when Europe was undergoing revolution. The political divisions in Colombia were similar to those in France and Germany. At that time, the social structure in Colombia must have had a great deal more in common with Europe's than has been the case since. At any rate, merchants, lawyers, artisans, and other "enlightened" individuals sought to create a political order which embodied economic liberty, a secular state, federalism, and democracy in Colombia, and this was the basis for the formation of the Liberal Party. Others resisted going so far, even though they supported democracy; they sought to preserve the scholastic tradition of Spain and looked back with favor on the peaceful and stable times of the colonial period. Only a few advocated a monarchy. These latter groups formed the Conservative Party.

Of the many issues that arose as some sought to set up a "modern" state, the controversy over the position of the Church was most persistent. German Colmenares (1968: 75) writes:

> Whoever wishes to define the very depth of the political controversies of the past century ought to have recourse to a quite simple antithesis. . . . The clean division between believers and "reds," between Catholics and the irreverant [sic] seems to contain the final cause *(rayón última)* of a passionate debate which unfolds into a sequence of additional points which concern tradition and modernity *(novedades)*, reaction and progress.

J. Lloyd Meacham (1966: 120) reports, "The Liberal Party, victorious in 1849 and remaining in the ascendancy with only short interruptions until 1880, promoted a vast 'democratic' program in which the Church was the principal sufferer." The Jesuits were expelled and divorce legalized, two policies which were later reversed by Conservative regimes. In 1861, the Church lands were expropriated. From that time on, the clergy opposed the Liberals and became involved in the partisan conflict at the local level. Only in the 1960s has the intense Conservative partisanship of the lower levels of the clergy ceased.

Extension of suffrage for all male citizens in local elections in 1886 and for national elections in 1910 and the periodic civil wars between the parties established intense party loyalties *(sectarismo)* among the masses. Aside from the clerical issue, it is doubtful that they understood the philosophical debates of their national leaders. The civil wars pushed the followers of the Liberal and Conservative ideologies into homogeneous communities. Orlando Fals Borda (1955: 241) describes how these communities formed into one region:

> When the two modern political parties, the Conservative and the Liberal, started to take full form during the 1860's, the Liberal bond became one of the social characteristics of Saucio (Cundinamarca). Then the peasants followed the dictates of *gamonales* who appeared to be *mayordomos,* or supervisors, for local landowners such as the Neiras, the Maldonados, the Corteses, and others.

Neighboring areas became Conservative through the same process. The electoral data from Boyacá, a department with small municipios, most dramatically shows the results. In 1949, a time of violence, 33 of the 110 municipios of Boyacá reported no opposition votes; 88 reported less than 10% for the opposition, be it Liberal or Conservative. The data from municipios does not show the full extent of the division because quite often the division was by the small rural community, the *vereda,* rather than by the larger municipio.

Colombia went through a period of fairly rapid economic and social change during the 1920s. Urban communities expanded; communication improved; labor unions formed. In order to maintain the two-party system, the parties had to accommodate the new conditions and ideas. The Liberal Party took on the cause of organized labor and began talking with a more equalitarian tone. Many of the young Liberals of the 1920s, for the most part sons of the elite and destined to become the party leaders in the 1940s, discussed advanced ideas at the Café Windsor, and some attended a marxist study group (Fals Borda, 1967: 107). The most extraordinary charismatic leader of the Liberal Party, Jorge Eliécer Gaitan, who by virtue of being of lower origins was not a full participant with the Windsor group, wrote his university thesis on "Las Ideas Socialistas en Colombia." The leadership of the Liberal Party was ready to preempt the intellectual ideas that a new party might have exploited. Needless to say, not all Liberal leaders made the turn to the left, and the party in its period of greatest electoral strength found itself divided.

Just as Colombia had imitated the ideological divisions that brought civil war to Europe in the mid-nineteenth century, it adopted the same divisions that brought civil war to Europe in the mid-twentieth century. As the Liberal Party took on socialist ideas, the Conservative Party followed the Falange of Spain, turning its opposition to socialism into a holy war. Increasingly in the 1940s, Laureano Gomez led the minority Conservatives into a noncompromising, no-holds-barred fight against the Liberals. As in the Liberal Party, not all the Conservative leaders followed the turn of the leading faction.

No one ever recorded what the peasants thought about these new ideas. One can deduce from their actions that the memories of the civil wars, the property that was won or lost, and the village priest were far more important than any abstract ideas. In 1930, 54% of the adult males voted in the highly contested elections. The Conservatives were demoralized and divided, giving the plurality of votes to the moderate Liberal leader, Enrique Olaya Herrera, who had the support of some moderate Conservatives. In spite of accommodation at that time at the national level, the Liberal peasants began attacks on the local Conservatives and the churches. After nearly 50 years of Conservative domination, the Liberals were more than ready to use the advantages of control of the national government to obtain local advantages.

As the two-party conflict increased in intensity in the 1930s and 1940s, it occurred in a country that, although it was 70% rural, in no way resembled the stereotype of passive and unmobilized peasants. The peasants were partisans and were quite willing to initiate action to take over land, molest or kill the members of the opposite party, or destroy churches.

The country had been politicized for a century, but the intensity of feeling increased considerably during the late 1940s. In the presidential election of 1946, the Liberal Party, divided by Gaitan, allowed the moderate Conservative Mariano Ospina Perez to win the presidency. Just as in 1930, the winning of power stimulated the partisans of the new government to attack the partisans of the old government (Guzman, 1968: 42-47). Violence in the countryside increased, and when Gaitan was assasinated in the streets of Bogota in 1948, the whole city broke into destructive riots. In the last free election for a decade, in April 1949, 74% of the males over 21 turned out to give the Liberals a solid majority in Congress. Presidential elections were scheduled for later that year, but the Conservative administration conducted such harassment and intimidation against the Liberal Party that the Liberals decided to withdraw from participation. Gomez won the uncontested elections.

The political career of Gaitan deserves mention because there are a number of striking similarities between his movement and that of Rojas' Anapo. Gaitan began and ended as a Liberal, but in between he formed a party, Union Nacional Izquierdista Revolucionaria (UNIR), which attacked both of the parties and the oligarchy that ruled them. Even while running for the presidency on one wing of the Liberal Party, he denounced "el pais politico," which he associated with the traditional leaders (Villaveces, 1968: 407-418). He received support from some progressive Conservatives (Fluharty, 1957: 82). His populist theme is well illustrated by the words with which he ended his campaign speeches:

People, for the moral restoration. To the charge.
People, for our victory. To the charge.
People, for the defeat of the oligarchy. To the charge.
People, for our victory. To the charge.

He denounced class divisions, but the masses responded more to his call than did the wealthy elite. German Arciniegas (1952: 79-80) says that Gaitan's appeal to the underprivileged nine-tenths was greater than that of any other South American political figure. In the 1946 presidential election, it is quite likely that the vote was divided along socioeconomic lines similarly to those in 1970.

The period of intentional depoliticization began in 1953, when the moderate Conservatives and Liberals encouraged the Minister of Defense, General Gustavo Rojas Pinilla, to take power. When Rojas took over on June 13, 1953, Vernon Lee Fluharty (1957: 139) reports:

Wild public jubilation greeted the downfall of Gomez. Liberals and Conservatives alike pledged support to the new government, in a great sigh of national relief. After five years of bloody strife, the peaceful transformation was all the more welcome, all the more dramatic.

Fluharty (1957) provides a very interesting constrast to the books on Colombia published both in Colombia and in the United States in the 1960s. He interpreted the convulsions of the 1940s as representing the quest of the masses for a new order and saw Rojas as responding to these desires. Since the National Front was created in 1958, very little of a positive nature has been published about Rojas, partly due to a disillusionment with his regime that set in during his last year in power, partly to the extent to which the upper class is able to dominate the press combined with the dependence of foreign scholars on this national press. Robert H. Dix's (1967: 124) very thorough description of Colombian politics states of Rojas:

> Rojas' vanity and ambition gave those who saw in the administration an opportunity for personal gain a wide field for flattery and for a weaving of the webs of corruption. A coterie formed whose connections permitted its members to establish economic empires. None were anxious [sic] for steps to be taken that might bring an early end to their preferment. Rojas himself was not immune to temptation. As one of his erstwhile supporters put it, Rojas might in fact have been his country's second Bolivar if he had not been so anxious to be its first rancher.

> Lacking both ideological direction and mass support, the single attempt at a "populistic authoritarian" solution to Colombia's crisis of the traditional order thus proved abortive.

If Dix's view had been believed and remembered by the Colombian masses, Rojas could never have made a comeback in popular and free elections.

Rojas came to power in 1953 because many had come to believe that the parties could not govern. He fell in 1957 because the parties had decided that they preferred an agreement between themselves to allowing Rojas to continue in power and destroy them. The Liberal leader, Alberto Lleras Comargo, proposed the formation of bipartisan opposition to Rojas in March 1956 and then went to Spain to reach agreement with the Conservative leader, Laureano Gomez. The result was the Declaration of Benidorm which called for the formation of a Civil Front. United action of business groups, labor unions, the Church, and students in May 1957 put pressure on the military to ask for the resignation of Rojas. The plebiscite of December 1957 gave popular endorsement to the National Front solution.

General Rojas had managed to reduce the level of violence but not eliminate it. Around 200,000 persons had been killed, and more would be killed in the 1960s, but the battle became less and less a battle between Conservatives and Liberals and more a fight of outlawry and revenge; in the 1960s it took on a more radical ideological tone (Guzman, 1968). The violence had changed the rural structure and culture by forcing migration within the rural area and to the cities. Some areas of intense violence shifted from Liberal majorities to almost 100% Conservative.

The partisan coalition of the Liberal and Conservative parties in the National Front gave the two parties a format in which they could discourage further acts of partisan violence and still maintain their positions in society. It also meant that they would have to consolidate their following on some other basis than "hereditary hatred," and that policy innovation would become more difficult. The National Front gave the parties another chance, but the founders of the system did not ask whether the system might not be so limiting that the parties could not survive beyond the sixteen years of the coalition.

THE NATIONAL FRONT AND THE TRADITIONAL PARTIES

Colombian society went through many profound changes in the 1950s and the 1960s as population increased at a rate over 3% a year, urbanization increased at 6% a year, radio receivers increased 12% a year, and motorized road and air transport broke the isolation of most of the villages and regional centers. These social changes called for new policies and forms of participation from the political parties, but at the same time, the National Front form of government inhibited party reform.

THE NATIONAL FRONT

The National Front took away one of the basic reasons for loyalty to a traditional party: opposition to the other party. The Front eliminated all electoral competition by stipulating that the presidency would be alternated between the parties. Seats on all representative bodies would be divided equally between the parties, regardless of number of votes received. This provision was carried to its logical extreme in some municipal councils where the populace was nearly 100% of one party. Certain persons became nominally of the other other party in order to fill the 50% of the seats allotted to that party. Administrative posts and ministries were also divided between the parties.

Since campaigns and elections were no longer directed against the other party, the infighting between factions of the same party at the department level became more intense. For instance, in the last days of the 1968 campaign, leaders of each faction accused the leaders of the other factions of misuse of funds, moral degeneration, and so on. Most factions are of a local or departmental level, and the different leaders compete to have their lists "promulgated" by the National Directorate as the "official" ones in a particular election. Persons included in the official list in one election may shift to a "dissident" list in the following election, which is almost always the result of factional infighting over places on the official list, and not of differences in point of view on policy. The Atlantic Coast departments are notorious for lack of discipline, and there are often as many as ten lists for each party.

The cement that held both of the traditional parties together was patronage. The fight between factions usually came out of their attempts to control more patronage, and the presence of patronage kept all the regular politicians loyal to the two parties. All governmental administrative positions—including teaching—are filled by patronage. Political leaders within the party are rewarded with control over patronage in accordance with their ability to bring in the party vote, especially for the national *Camara* and *Senado*. To become a national leader, it is almost mandatory to show continuous electoral strength at the departmental level. Electoral strength will bring an appointment as governor, mayor of a major municipio, or a ministerial position.

Before 1970, congressional elections were held at a different time than were the presidential elections. The importance of these elections was demonstrated by the fact that more people turned out to vote for senators at the congressional elections every four years than turned out to vote for the president. Both Camara and Senado seats are divided by the electoral quotient system, with the number of Senado seats being slightly more than half that of the Camara. The total party vote in a department is divided by the number of seats allocated to that department party to determine the quotient. This quotient is then divided into the vote for the different lists. The dividend is the number of seats won by the list. The seat or seats remaining go to lists according to the highest residual vote. The candidates win elections according to their rank order on the list; the voter must vote the whole list and cannot change the order of the candidates.

The intense competition for elected seats provides the substance of Colombian politics. Many party leaders have recognized that reforms of government, party, and programs are necessary in order to maintain the position of the two parties and of those who have been enjoying the game of traditional party politics. Carlos Lleras (1966: 78-79) stated the problem most explicitly: "We all have at times the impression that the blood is congealing in the old party veins. We must inject a new fluid if they are not to be obstructed and die." Lleras, however, has little time to devote to party work as he has been involved in government with the unending task of trying to patch together compromises within and between the two parties. Attempts at change have been made in both organization and party programs, but all attempts have met with the obstacle of factional politics.

PARTY ORGANIZATION

The organization at the base of the two traditional political parties has been and is made up of local chieftains called *gamonales,* who are either born into this position or are connected to local families with wealth and prestige (Santa, 1964: 74-78). These hereditary leaders organize the local campaigns and dispense patronage and other rewards. The regional leadership consisting of these local gamonales is to a great extent hereditary, but certain families compete for regional leadership and provide the basis of factional politics. The national leadership is also to a great extent hereditary. Ex-President Mariano Ospina, the strongest leader of the Conservative Party, is descended from one of the first Colombian presidents. Alvaro Gomez succeeded his father, another ex-President. Alfonso Lopez Michelson, presently one of the top three Liberal leaders, is the son of another President. The system is not completely closed, however, and an occasional leader may work his way up (Payne, 1968a).

This traditional system lacks a popular base. The local leaders mobilize, but they are responsible neither to the population nor to the national leadership in any real way. The party is a confederation, and a national leader who wants to make reforms must negotiate with the local leaders, most of whom are not interested in national programs not tied to additional promotion, patronage, and other benefits (Payne, 1968b).

The Liberal Party recognized in its party statutes of 1963 that it was important to establish a popular base (Lleras, 1963: 806). Party members were to pay dues and receive membership cards, and local party leaders would be elected by the members. But the party found that the local leaders gave membership cards to their loyal followers and maintained their control as before, so the party returned to the traditional system. In serarching for another way of including persons aside from the traditional political class, the Liberal Party had representatives of established interest groups attend the party nominating convention in 1968. This method had very little impact in most areas in 1968 and 1970. The nominating convention majority was made up of the municipal councilmen, who were in no way responsible to a popular base.

The most successful attempt to break with the traditional party organization has come from the Conservative Party in the Department of Antioquia, where J. Emilio Valderama has established a popular base by setting up a "cellular" organization within each of the *barrios* and its subdivisions, each organization forming an active center for study groups, conventions, and social services such as health centers and schools. He declared in *El Siglo* of October 30, 1967, that, a modern party ought to have the organization of a business firm, because in the end it is called upon to produce for Colombia the human article endowed with capacity, honesty, and competence in order to accelerate economic development.

The Conservative Party claims to be trying to extend this organization to the rest of the country.

Interrelated with the problem of organization is the problem of party finance, on which we failed to obtain data. However, interviews with some national leaders and several Valle leaders provide general information: while the Conservative Party has some revenue from a building it owns in Bogota, the basic sources of funds for both parties are donations by government employees, and the candidates' own contributions. Wealthy aspirants are able to obtain good positions on the list by promising to pay for expenses above and beyond their own campaigns. The poverty of the party at the national level makes it nearly impossible for national leaders to use funds to influence the local nominations or campaigns.

PARTY PROGRAMS

The National Front has limited the extent to which party programs could be shaped. The major policy pronouncements of the National Front period have not come from the parties, but from the biparty group which was brought together to organize the presidential campaign. In 1962, the two parties agreed on a Program of the National Front, still their basic position (Lleras, 1963: 596), stating their aims to be:

> to obtain peace between the parties, perfect the democratic institutions, stimulate economic development and forge the structure of a modern society, not divided by the tremendous inequalities that now divide it and which offers to all its members remunerative labor, a satisfactory standard of living, protected against risks with free access to culture and the opportunity to achieve the highest positions both in private and public business.

In 1965, the National Front partners responded to the complaint that it was organized to preserve the status quo by registering another major program statement and renaming it the Front of National Transformation. When the political parties have elaborated independent statements, as did the Liberal Party in October 1967, these statements have become the basis for neither a political campaign nor a governmental program. The principal theme of the official wings of the two parties has been simply to support the National Front government.

The major national dissident factions of the two parties have provided the only other policy initiatives. Alfonso Lopez Michelson, the son of the Liberal president who initiated many changes in the 1930s, formed the principal national dissident faction of the Liberal Party in the 1960s. He protested from the very beginning of the National Front against the provisions which gave the Conservative Party, which he considered a minority party, equal rights with the Liberals, and against the alternation of the presidency between parties. He developed a following and established a newspaper, *la Calle*, in order to promote the cause of "popular Liberalism," as opposed to oligarchical Liberalism. In 1960, the group organized into the Movimiento Revolucionario Liberal (MRL) and established separate electoral lists. Throughout the 1960s, this faction expressed the danger to the Liberal Party of being identified with the bipartisan compromises of the National Front. They wanted to maintain the identity of the party as a group which sought reforms for and protected the interests of the popular classes. They sought stronger measures of land and tax reform and urged closer cooperation with Cuba and the other Communist states. The movement found its greatest support in those Liberal rural areas which had suffered most from the violence. In Cali, they developed support among some of the poorer sectors by organizing urban land invasions. Their electoral support peaked with 36% of the Liberal vote in 1962, when a Conservative was the official candidate for the presidency, and declined steadily thereafter. The MRL became formally reunited with the Liberal Party in October 1967. The convention which formalized the union issued a program of "accion Liberal" which embodied many points previously stressed by the MRL.

During the first eight years of the National Front, the Conservative Party was divided into two factions of almost equal size, both of which supported the National Front. The followers of Laureano Gomez were somewhat less cooperative than the Mariano Ospina faction. However, with the election of Carlos Lleras to the presidency in 1966, the followers of Gomez, now organized by Alvaro Gomez Hurtado after the death of his father in 1965, refused to cooperate with the National Front because they claimed that Carlos Lleras was governing too much as a liberal. Thus, they took it upon themselves to preserve a conservative identity by almost completely opposing Lleras and most of his government's initiatives. They particularly opposed tax and land reform and minor attempts to initiate a family planning program. The *Alvaristas* failed to maintain support and dropped from 27% of the Conservative vote in 1966 to 17% in 1968. (Anapo getting 31 and 28% of the total Conservative vote). In June of 1969, agreement was reached to reunify the independents with the Ospina wing of the party, and the documents were signed on July 3. At that point, however, Belesario Betancur split in order to form a new dissident group with a more progressive image.

THE PRESIDENTIAL NOMINATION CONVENTIONS

The Conservative Party had to preserve its unity in the 1970 presidential election in order to have a certain amount of autonomy vis à vis the Liberals and to defeat the opposition candidacy of Rojas Pinilla. Instead, the party's organizational chaos caused a three-way split. The Liberal Party, for which the situation was far less critical, split along the same lines.

Cooperation with the Liberals posed one of the problems for the Conservatives. It has been clear for several years that the Liberals were grooming Misael Pastrana Borrero for the presidency. He had served as the most important minister in the Carlos Lleras government before his resignation to become Ambassador to Washington, which made him eligible for the candidacy. Ex-President Mariano Ospina, who had negotiated for the Conservatives with Lleras on all important matters was known to be also backing Pastrana. Many Conservatives, however did not like the idea of the Liberals making the choice for them, as in 1963 when the Conservatives had not been able to agree.

Belisario Betancur did not wait for the Conservative convention to proclaim himself a candidate. With strong support from the labor unions, developed when he was Minister of Labor in the Valencia administration, the backing of ex-President Valencia, and a good following in the Liberal Party, he decided that he would openly challenge Ospina's control of the party. He might have gathered the support from the Conservative convention if he had tried, but he chose to ignore the opportunity.

The Conservative convention met in early November to make its choice on the nomination. The 536 delegates included ex-presidents, ex-ministers, ex-governors, senators, representatives, deputies, and special delegations of workers, students, and women. The credential committee, in attempting to decide who were true Conservatives, excluded all the followers of Rojas and Betancur. None of the delegates had had occasion to consult with the Conservative masses on their presidential preferences; instead, they represented the department and national political chieftains. Ospina, who had personally intervened in most of the departmental Conservative conventions in 1968 and who had seen his "official" lists come out ahead in that election, chaired the convention and controlled the largest group of delegates.

The anti-Ospina groups were behind a large number of "pre-candidates." Alvaro Gomez, who was not a precandidate, but who controlled the largest uncommitted faction, avoided taking sides; his followers divided. The "syndicate," as the opposition to Ospina was called, met and decided to pool forces to back Evaristo Sourdis, ex-minister and senator from the Atlantic Coast. When the first ballot was counted, Sourdis came out ahead of Pastrana by four votes.

After tedious secret negotiations by the leaders of the different factions, the convention finally decided to submit two names to the Liberal convention. The Liberal convention, well controlled by Carlos Lleras, chose Pastrana. Despite the Liberal decision, Sourdis decided to maintain his candidacy. The Liberal Party broke along the same lines as the Conservatives, becoming *Pastranistas, Belisaristas,* or *Sourdistas.* The differing factions thus chose to risk a victory by their common enemy, Rojas Pinilla.

LOSS OF SUPPORT FOR THE TRADITIONAL PARTIES

The leaders of the two traditional parties have on the whole failed to "inject a new fluid" into the parties, and the blood has continued to congeal. The parties in 1970 were, as they had been in the 1940s, loose organizations of local political leaders with real ties neither to the masses nor to the national leadership. As a result, their popular support has progressively declined, as indicated by the electoral abstention record. Abstention is itself an ambiguous act. Except for political surveys, it is impossible to distinguish between abstainers who are apathetic and those who are alienated. Its relation to Colombian political parties is more direct, however, for the parties' primary role is to bring out the vote. This they have failed to do.

During the 1940s, the two traditional parties were drawing well over 40% of the potential vote. The peak turnout came in 1949, with 74% of the electorate. With the institution of the National Front and female suffrage, the two parties received 60% of the expanded electorate in 1958 (Table 1). From 1964 to 1970, they received between 27 and 31% of the potential vote. In other words, less than half the percentage of the electorate which had voted for them in 1958 was still doing so 10 years later.

In years when a Conservative is running for the presidency or is in office, the Liberal vote has fallen off more than has the Conservative vote. When a Liberal is running for the presidency or is in office, the Conservative vote has dropped more. In 1970, both traditional parties

TABLE 1
PERCENTAGE OF ADULT POPULATION VOTING
(as percentage of total electorate)

	1958	1960	1962	1964	1966	1968	1970
Liberals	35	23	25	16	20	15	17
Conservatives	25	16	19	11	11	10	12
Subtotal	60	39	44	27	31	25	29
ANAPO			1.6	4	7	6	16
Total voting	60	39	45	31	38	31	46

were attracting about half the electoral support that they had attracted in the past. As 1970 was a year when only Conservatives were running for the presidency, it is possible that the Liberal vote has held up slightly better than the Conservative.

Table 2 shows the vote for the two traditional parties by department in order of the degree of violence the department suffered in the last 25 years. The only department which has had intense violence and is not low in votes is Huila, where Misael Pastrana, the official candidate, is from. These data support Camilo Torres' (1970: 511) prediction that the traditional party leaders would not be able to sustain their positions where armed conflict had developed new leadership:

> The structure of peasant leadership changed with the onset of violence. The charismatic leaders of the *vereda* grew in importance with respect to the leaders of the town or county seat. When the traditional leaders and the *gamonal* leaders—large landowners operating within a feudal-style latifundism as local political leaders—of the towns were obedient to the institutions responsible for violence against the peasants, they lost their positions of leadership among

TABLE 2
VOTE FOR TRADITIONAL PARTIES BY DEPARTMENT

Department	Percentage of Electorate	Department	Percentage of Electorate
More Violence		**Less Violence**	
Valle	24	Cundinamarca	30
Tolima	27	Norte de Santander	32
Huila	41	Cauca	30
Quindio	21	Cordoba	31
Santander	26	Guajira	35
Meta	19	Magdalena	40
Boyacá	26	Nariño	32
Cesar	21	Chocó	41
Antioquia	22	Bolivar	36
Risaralda	30	Atlantico	36
Caldas	33		

them. The same thing happened to the charismatic leaders, who were therefore no longer such in the true sense of the word.

Urbanization had a similar result. When the population moved to the urban centers, they moved away from the hereditary political leaders. Without the pressures of the traditional setting, the population no longer turned out to vote in such numbers. Bogota turned out 29% of the electorate for the traditional parties in 1970, but Medillin and Cali turned out only 22 and 20% respectively.

The preelectoral survey in the Department of Valle gives added evidence on the loss of traditional party strength. The self-identification with one of the traditional parties is still stronger than the vote. Seventy-two percent of these interviewed said they belonged to a political party, and 66% named either Liberal or Conservative. Only 2% said they belonged to Anapo, which at that time had not yet declared itself a political party. Much of the Anapo vote, then, came from persons who named themselves as Liberals (21% of Liberals in Valle) or as Conservatives (31% of Conservatives in Valle). The generational shift from parents of Liberals to children of Conservatives is small (7.2%), and of parents of Conservatives to children of Liberals is likewise small (7.4%). On the other hand the number of children whose parents were of one party but who do not themselves identify with one of the traditional parties or the National Front is large (23.8% with Liberal parents and 23.4% with Conservative parents). The loss is not made up for by persons whose parents did not belong to any party or whose party affiliation was unknown. From these data, the net loss in party affiliation from parent to children for all parties comes to 13.1%.

The party attrition is shown in much more striking proportions when those whose parents belonged to a party but do not themselves are listed by age and location on Table 3. The older persons in all areas have tended

TABLE 3
GENERATION PARTY ATTRITION: ADULTS WITH NO PARTY AFFILIATION WHOSE PARENTS BELONGED TO A PARTY[a]

	Rural	n	Town	n	Cali	n
21-25	32.4	37	27.9	43	47.3	93
26-30	22.6	31	18.2	44	44.4	148
31-40	20.7	87	14.5	110	43.3	298
41-50	18.5	54	14.8	88	28.5	200
51-60	25.6	39	10.4	48	19.1	113
60	26.3	19	7.4	27	11.5	52

a. Percentage of all who had parents belonging to party by age and location.

to maintain an allegiance to a party, but only half the young people in Cali, even though their parents were party members, are willing to consider themselves as a member of a party. The persons in the rural area show little difference between age groups. However, the younger adults in the towns are also more likely to give up a claim to a party.

GOVERNMENT POLICY AND ECONOMIC CONDITIONS

Our studies showed, as have studies in other places, that voters respond to a great extent to what the government is doing for them and to their general living conditions. Furthermore, these governmental programs and the economic situation provide the raw material of the electoral campaigns. It does not matter to the people that both the size of the programs and the state of the economy, expecially in less-developed countries, are often beyond the control of the government. The Colombian government accomplished much of what it agreed to do under the Alliance for Progress and received a large amount of foreign assistance, but our surveys showed that 50% of the people felt conditions had not improved and even more were unenthusiastic about the programs of the Lleras administration.

THE GOVERNMENT PROGRAMS

The major restriction on what the government could do either in promoting economic development or in redistributing income was its limited ability to mobilize resources. When total government revenues are totaled, including those of the autonomous agencies and local government, they come to only a little more than $50 U.S. per person. The low level has two causes: a per capita product of under $300 U.S. and a tax capacity of only about 10% of GNP (other revenue comes primarily from payment for services). Jorgen R. Lotz and Elliott R. Morss (1967) measured the tax effort in Colombia from the residual after taking per capita GNP and the size of the foreign sector into account and found that Colombia ranked 39 out of 52 developing countries. In addition to a low tax effort, the Colombian tax system is income inelastic, meaning that as income and inflation rise, taxes rise less than proportionately. Furthermore, taxes depend to a great extent on the level of imports and exports, sectors which have declined or stagnated throughout most of the National Front period. In short, the Colombian government has had to make a continuous effort in order to hold its low level of tax income (Bird, 1970: 33).

One of its first acts when the Rojas Pinilla government took power in 1953 was to make the "most important income tax reform of the post-war period" (Bird, 1970: 192-193), increasing tax rates on high incomes and corporations and taxing individual dividends for the first time.

One of the National Front government's first acts after taking power in 1958 was to modify the income tax laws by increasing exemptions, which both reduced the total tax take and decreased the progressivity of the tax. The OAS mission under Milton Taylor (Taylor, 1965: 221-224) calculated that the lowest quartile of income receivers paid 10.9% of their income in taxes and the highest quartile paid 12.7% of their income in taxes. When President Carlos Lleras was seeking to make tax reforms in 1967, he revealed that many large income receivers were paying no taxes at all. He sought to have the taxes paid by individuals published, but withdrew the threat under vociferous protest from the wealthy. In 1965, the Valencia administration decreased the progressivity of the tax system through the introduction of a sales tax.

The Lleras government made more progress on the tax front than had previous administrations, managing to mobilize a somewhat larger share of the nation's resources through the sales tax, a new gasoline tax, improved tax administration, and an improved import situation. Central government taxes increased from 7.1% of the GNP in the 1963-1965 period to 8.8% in 1969 (Inter-American Development Bank, 1970: 167). The system became no more progressive, and may have become less so through the withholding of income taxes of the working and middle classes. It is doubtful that any other political leadership could have accomplished more in the political system of the National Front. What was done, however, was enough to give the government the ability neither to mobilize sufficient resources for a major impact on development nor to redistribute income through the fiscal system.

In the absence of any large increase in tax revenues, the development efforts of the National Front governments were greatly dependent upon foreign aid resources. Both the Alberto Lleras (1958-1962) and the Carlos Lleras (1966-1970) administrations were considered among the better hopes for the Alliance for Progress and received large loans and grants from the various development assistance agencies. The Guillermo Valencia administration, on the other hand, ran into considerable disagreement with the assistance agencies over the kind of economic reforms it should undertake, primarily disagreement about exchange rates and control of inflation, and aid was reduced for nearly two years (U.S. Senate, 1969). Overall, Colombia received commitments equal to 4.0% of its GDP between mid-1961 and mid-1969, placing it seventh among Latin

American countries in receipt of assistance (McCamant, 1971). Net receipts were, of course, lower and for 1960-1967 came to 1.9% of GDP. With central government saving averaging 3.8% of GDP, one can conclude that investments controlled by the Central Government were increased by approximately 50% due to foreign aid. The funds allowed an increase in hydroelectric production, road investments, home and school construction, and rural and industrial credit. The assistance allowed the economy, with its critical foreign exchange shortage, to operate at a level closer to its capacity. The increase in foreign finance in 1968 and 1969 to around 6% of GDP undoubtedly was a major factor in the increase in economic growth in those years.

Foreign aid had a major impact on the level of investments, but it did not in any way affect the question of redistribution. Land reform was called for by the Charter of Punta del Este, but foreign aid has not been used to encourage land reform. Land invasions, rural violence, massive migration to the urban areas while land is underutilized, low growth in production of agricultural products, rural poverty, all indicate that land redistribution is a major need in Colombia (Duff, 1968; Havens and Flinn, 1970; Smith, 1967). The Colombian government recognized the need in laws passed in 1936 and 1961. In writing the law of 1961, the Alberto Lleras government bypassed Congress and went to a nonpartisan Agrarian Reform Committee, chaired by Carlos Lleras and containing prestigious members from many sectors of the society (Duff, 1968: 42-61). The bill met with strong opposition from the well-organized interests of large landholders, *Sociedad de Agricultores Colombianos* and *Federacion Nacional de Cafeteros,* and the *Laureanista* wing of the Conservative Party carried on the attack against it in Congress. The law as passed placed emphasis on encouraging the use of uncultivated land rather than the redistribution of land under cultivation. Land could be acquired through the enforcement of the 1936 law which stated that land not cultivated within ten years would revert to the state. If cultivated land were expropriated, 20% of the value was to be paid in cash and the remainder in 4% bonds.

Success of land reform depended upon the vigor of the administration of the law. The Valencia government took over shortly after it was passed, but a Liberal was left in charge of INCORA. However, INCORA did not receive the funds called for by the law, and President Valencia refused to sign any expropriation decrees. INCORA devoted most of its resources to developing irrigation projects and agricultural credit. When Carolos Lleras became President in 1966, INCORA received more executive support. Nevertheless, its efforts remained primarily technical rather than redistributive. The result, as summed up by the Inter-American Development Bank (1970: 173) was,

> Between 1961 and September, 1969, 617 families were benefited by land programs covering 20,500 acres which had come under Government control, and 5,155 families received 175,000 acres through land purchases and expropriation from private parties.

One of the few estates expropriated was that of Gustavo Rojas Pinilla. The number of families benefited by land redistribution would be no more than 0.4% of all rural families. About ten times as many families benefited through acquiring titles to land, presumably land which they already occupied. The outcome of land reform efforts, then, was minimal. Land distribution was not made more equal, and the number of landless increased.

In order to organize stronger support behind land reform and other agricultural policies, President C. Lleras issued a decree in May, 1967, that directed the Minister of Agriculture to promote the organization of *usuarios,* or users of government services in the rural areas (see *El Tiempo* for May 6, 1967). Any peasant who used or wished to use agricultural credit, irrigation, land, extension services, or any other kind of service could register and become a member of the Association of Usuarios. The Counselor to the President, José Galat, described the situation that the government wished to overcome, as reported in *El Tiempo* of May 6, 1967, "The peasant masses have been pushed aside *(marginadas)* from the state entities which wish to protect and help them by the beligerance of the *gamonales* who wish to preserve the atomization of the population."

In 1971, after more than a million peasants had registered as usuarios, the United Nations Food and Agricultural Organization (1971: 152) stated in a report on land reform in Latin America, "It is probable that, when historians analyze the whole period of the National Front, they will find that the most important fact of the period has been the birth of the peasant organizations." By 1970 and 1971, the Association of Usuarios had the organization to back the efforts of INCORA in land expropriation and to urge the government to do more. In a few areas, the Association of Usuarios provided the vehicle for the election of peasant leaders to Congress (UNFAO, 1971: 154). The presidential candidates, especially the official candidate Misael Pastrana, made considerable efforts to court this newly organized group.

Much of the time and effort of the C. Lleras administration was devoted to pushing a constitutional reform through Congress to reorganize the powers and structure of government. The issue was not one that the masses of the population could follow. The preelectoral survey in Valle asked persons about one point in the constitutional reform which pertained to that election—namely, the reinstitution of free party competition at the local level—and it turned out only eight percent of the sample knew the correct answer. If the constitutional reform had any direct impact on citizens' evaluation of the government, it was only in a very vague and symbolic way. On the other hand, the reform was important in Liberal Party politics. The leader of the MRL, Alfonso Lopez M., and President Lleras found a wide area of agreement on this reform issue. Lopez had expressed his view in a book in 1966, *El Estado Fuerte,* in which he had called for constitutional change that would allow for stronger executive leadership. The constitutional reform effort, then, provided a basis for cooperation between the dissident liberal faction and the government and contributed to the reunification of the Liberal Party in 1967.

The many and complex points of the reform were presented in three blocks. The first simply called for a widening of the scope of government authority in principle. The second reorganized the powers of Congress and the Executive. The third eased the transition from the coalition form of government to that of free competition. The President felt that these changes were necessary if the government was going to be able to organize the economy and promote economic development. President Lleras, who once gave Congress his resignation when it failed to pass one block, did not have the benefit of these constitutional reforms until the very end of his administration, as they were not finally passed until December 1968. (Congress refused to accept the resignation; the previous defeat had been made possible by the defection of some traditional Liberals, anxious to preserve their prerogatives.)

Another field which President Carlos Lleras handled with some finesse was foreign policy. He disarmed all of his critics by coming down on all sides at once: he demonstrated Colombia's independence by defying the International Monetary Fund on exchange policy and developing trade relations with Eastern Europe; he kept on good terms with the United States and the international financial institutions by stabilizing the economy and making no symbolic attacks on U.S. or foreign investment. When he received a major loan, he claimed it demonstrated international confidence in his economic policy. He seized the role of Latin American leader by convening a meeting of Latin American presidents in Bogota to organize the Andean group within the Latin American Free Trade Association. He mollified the Conservatives by hosting the Eucharistic Conference in 1968 with the first visit of any Pope to Latin America. His personal style may have been as important as his policies. This short, soft-spoken leader gave periodic *charlas* on radio and television and took weekend tours of the country as a fatherly school teacher-type who was continuously studying the problems of the people and presenting solutions for them in speeches which were long and tedious but covered his programs point by point. In the last year of his administration, his image was somewhat tarnished by a scandal involving his Minister of Agriculture, Enrique Peñalosa, who was accused of using his office to give contracts from which he benefited.

In both 1968 and 1970, we asked respondents for an evaluation of the programs of President Lleras, and although the question was worded differently, there is sufficient similarity to make a comparison. In 1968, 67% said that they thought President Lleras has provided good programs for the country. In the postelectoral survey in 1970, only 42% classified his government as good or very good (see Table 4).

A comparison of the response by class provides support for the conclusion that the drop was due to real differences rather than to the wording of the question. Taking an answer of good or very good in 1970 to correspond to yes in 1968, the evaluation of the upper class dropped by 6%, the middle class by 4%, the working class by 30%, and the lower class by 22%. This evaluation indicates that government popularity is not solely a result of national economic growth, for economic conditions improved considerably in the last two years of the Lleras administration. The lower evaluation may have been caused by the harsh criticisms levied against the government by the Anapo campaign. Those who voted for Rojas were far

TABLE 4
EVALUATION OF PRESIDENT C. LLERAS' PROGRAMS
(in percentages)

	Upper-Class	Middle-Class	Working-Class	Lower-Class	Weighted Average
Do you think that President Lleras has provided good programs for the country? (1968)					
Yes	86	66	74	55	67
No	8	25	15	28	21
Don't know	6	9	11	17	12
How would you classify the government of Carlos Lleras R.? (1970)					
Very good	55	25	11	8	13
Good	35	37	33	25	29
Not so good[a]	15	24	36	39	35
Bad	4	12	12	20	16
Don't know	1	2	8	8	7

a. **Regular** in Spanish.

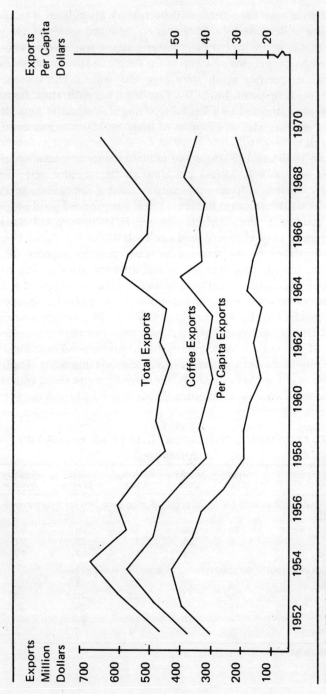

Figure 1: COLOMBIAN EXPORT TRENDS

more critical of Lleras than those who voted for the other nonofficial candidates or who abstained.

THE ECONOMIC SITUATION

When the government has only limited resources with which to affect the economy, living conditions become more dependent upon other economic factors, the most important of which in Colombia is coffee. One of the most important facts to know in order to understand the outcome of the 1970 elections is the trend of coffee export values, which is portrayed on Figure 1. General Rojas was president when coffee prices were high, but the National Front has faced lower prices throughout its rule. Total coffee exports averaged $500.4 million annually during the Rojas administration and $339.0 million during the years of the National Front. Other exports expanded during the National Front period but not enough to make up for falling coffee exports and the increase in the population. The per capita value of exports in current dollars averaged $48 during the Rojas administration and $29 during the National Front. With declining or stagnating exports, all economic problems became more difficult. Both taxes and the overall level of the economy depend on the level of exports. The fall of export values in 1956 and 1957 weakened the Rojas government and generated inflation, but after Rojas' fall, the situation continued to deteriorate. By 1970, the fact that the Rojas period looked good to many persons in comparison with the 1960s was constantly repeated by the Rojas campaign.

The weak export sector did not bring economic growth completely to a halt. During 1960-1965, the gross domestic product grew by 4.9% annually, or 1.4% per capita. During 1965-1969, it grew by 5.2% or 1.7% per capita. However, during much of the period, industry had to operate below capacity because of the restrictions on the import of semi-manufactured materials. The balance of payments was perpetually in trouble, and the government had to undertake repeated devaluations of the peso, an act that always raised howls of protest, for devaluation and the loss of government revenue, resulting in government deficits, generated inflation, which meant that wage and salary earners had trouble maintaining their past level of living. The annual rate of inflation went above 20% in the middle 1960s, but the C. Lleras government pursued strong anti-inflationary measures and brought the rate down to 8% in 1969.

The slow rate of economic growth in Colombia during the 1960s did not absorb the growing labor force brought by a 3.2% annual population growth rate. The International Labor Organization estimated that one-

TABLE 5
IMPROVEMENT IN CONDITIONS OF LIFE, 1968 AND
1970, BY CLASS, CALI[a]

Year	Upper	Middle	Working	Lower	Total
1968	79.0	50.0	50.0	40.0	48.0
1970	82.9	58.0	46.8	45.7	49.2

a. Percentage answering yes.

quarter of the labor force in Colombia is underutilized (Ginnold, 1971). The open rate of unemployment in the cities was approximately 14% during the slack year of 1967 with another estimated 7% not looking for jobs because of their scarcity. The situation improved with the economic expansion of 1969 and 1970, and the Colombian Statistical Institute estimated that open unemployment had fallen in Bogota to 9.6% in 1970. The official statistics, everyone admits, tend to understate the problem.

In 1968 and again in 1970 in the preelectoral survey, the interviewee was asked if he felt that living conditions had improved during the National Front. Table 5 shows the results by class. While 48% of the respondents in 1968 felt that living conditions had improved, 49.2% of the respondents in 1970 still felt that conditions had improved. The difference between classes in Cali is striking. Eighty-three percent of the upper class stated that conditions had improved, but only 46% of the working and lower classes thought so.

Tables 6 and 7 show how improvement in living conditions is related to location, age, length of residence, and education. Education had to be used in the rural areas and towns as a reflection of social status. The relationship of education remains constant in all areas, and the group with a university education has about 30% more who state that conditions have improved than those with no education. However, in rural areas there seems to be little difference between those with no school and those with

TABLE 6
CONDITIONS OF LIFE DURING THE NATIONAL FRONT
BY LOCATION AND AGE, VALLE[a]

Age	Rural	Town	Cali
21-25	40.4	51.9	39.5
26-30	54.2	45.5	43.9
31-40	46.8	59.7	49.0
41-50	62.7	61.1	53.6
51-60	81.3	68.8	56.2
Over 60	48.3	59.5	59.2
Total	54.8	58.8	49.2

a. Percentage who say conditions improved in 1970.

 apologdes e

TABLE 7
PERCENTAGE SAYING LIVING CONDITIONS HAD IMPROVED
DURING NATIONAL FRONT BY PLACE, LENGTH
OF RESIDENCE AND EDUCATION[a]

	0-2 Years	3-4 Years	5-14 Years	15 Years	All of Life	Total	n
Cali							
0			35.0	34.6	33.3	35.4	65
P1-2	38.5		33.3	41.3	45.5	38.7	129
P3-5	39.5	36.0	44.2	51.0	51.6	47.4	598
S1-3			45.5	53.4	62.3	54.4	180
S4-6	81.8		67.7	75.0	58.3	65.4	107
Univ.				61.5	85.7	73.8	65
Total	55.7	38.0	45.1	51.6	54.7	49.9	
n	79	50	370	376	276	1,151	
Town							
0	30.8				35.7	37.2	43
P1-2	33.3		53.8	61.1	61.5	54.8	73
P3-5	46.2	60.0	59.3	56.9	67.1	60.0	245
S1-3			50.0	53.3	87.5	63.0	73
S4-6					83.3	69.0	29
Univ.						62.5	16
Total	38.2	61.1	56.3	56.0	68.5	58.1	
n	68	18	112	116	168	482	
Rural							
0			60.0	58.3	45.5	54.0	37
P1-2	38.5		53.8	66.7	48.0	50.0	70
P3-5	39.3		48.8	61.8	53.4	52.5	202
S1-3					72.7	67.8	28
S4-6						82.3	17
Univ.							7
Total	47.5	65.2	51.3	65.1	53.8	54.9	
n	59	23	76	63	143	364	

a. Percentage given only when number in category was ten or greater.

primary education. The situation improves greatly for those with a secondary education. The length of time a person has resided in the municipio has a different effect in different locations. In Cali, the largest percentage for whom conditions had not improved was among those who came to Cali between three and fifteen years ago, or during the later stage of the violence. The difference, however, is only 10%. On the other hand, in the towns and the rural areas, the new migrants are much less likely (20%) to say that conditions have improved. Age also makes a difference of about 20% in all areas, the youngest being the most dissatisfied. In the towns and rural areas, those over sixty are not as likely to say that conditions have improved as those slightly younger. Since the younger are also better educated, the difference in both education and age is understated. Those under thirty with little or no education are the ones most likely to feel conditions have not improved.

In a later section, the responses to the questions about the evaluation of the Lleras government and living conditions will be related to the voting patterns of the 1970 elections. First, it is necessary to show how the Anapo movement exploited these issues. Its strength did not arise from worsening conditions in the last few years; if anything, the situation had improved. Rather, the Anapo movement attracted people who were already dissatisfied and were ready to be mobilized. Rojas politicized the discontent.

THE ANAPO MOVEMENT

Why did those whose ties to the traditional parties were weakening and those who found their living conditions worsening decide to vote for Rojas for president? They could have abstained, as many of them had in previous years and as they were being urged to by the radical priests and other discontents. One wonders, too, whether the vote was a simple protest that would evaporate as conditions changed or if it represented a new commitment. What had the Anapo movement done to attract their vote? Was the attraction of Anapo the charisma of its leader, Gustavo Rojas Pinilla or was it the appeal of the program? Did Anapo weave a coalition of previously organized groups or did it achieve its own organization with activists committed to it?

General Rojas and the Anapo movement are similar to Juan Peron and his movement in Argentina, for Rojas attempted to imitate Peron in many ways while he was in power. Both populist movements appealed to the working class and poor without evoking marxist dogma. On closer analysis, however, the timing and manner in which the movements developed was quite different. Peron built his following, before and during his presidency, basing it on organized labor. Rojas left the presidency without an organized following. He had come to power not on his own doing but at the request of leaders in both traditional parties who asked him to manage their conflict. His administration contained both his own men and those who owed allegiance to the traditional parties, and his attempts at organizing popular forces were without any real success. He tried to develop labor support through the *Confederacion Nacional de Trabajadores,* affiliated with the peronist Latin American labor movement, ATLAS, and later, after it disbanded at the time of the fall of Peron, through the *Gran Central Obrera.* Neither group got very far in proselytizing workers within the older labor conferations which were tied to the traditional parties. Rojas' attempts to organize a political party developed no mass support. He set up the *Moviemiento de Acción Nacional* in 1954, and after it died, he tried again with the *Third Force*. When he resigned in May 1957, no civilian group existed that could have organized a large popular protest in his favor.

Rojas did feel, however, that the Army would support him, in spite of the fact that its highest officers had asked him to resign. Shortly after he returned from Spain in 1958, the government arrested him and fifty of his followers for a plot which would have been initiated by bands of terrorists and followed by military intervention (Martz, 1962: 281). In October 1961, a group of army officers was arrested and accused of attempting to lead an uprising to place Rojas in power. In August 1963, Rojas was arrested again and accused of plotting to overthrow the Valencia government. Following the congressional elections in 1964, he explained his position to correspondent Richard Eder (1964), expressing confidence that Anapo could win the next elections, "but the people cannot wait two years for a change. I have been holding them back and will continue to do so as long as I can, but if it proves impossible, I shall have to put myself at their lead." Rojas expressed a preference for a military rebellion and indicated that while the top military was against him, "from major on down, almost all of the officers are with me."

General Rojas did not seem to have the ability to arouse the civilian masses, for he was not a politician and had never participated in an election before 1962. He had attended military schools and studied engineering at Angola Tri-State College in Indiana. He had proved successful in gaining promotions in the Army, but his only nonmilitary experience before assuming the presidency came when he served briefly as Minister of Communications. John Martz (1962: 243) gives a negative account of his political ability while in power:

> Public appearances, although not infrequent, were somewhat formal affairs at which he was surrounded by sober-faced aides and armed guards. When addressing the nation, he spoke over the radio rather than haranguing the crowd from the palace balcony. Indeed, when he tried to whip up the passions of his audience, he failed dismally. . . . Added to Rojas Pinilla's failures as a demagogue, then, were his shortcomings as a politician. Perhaps the greatest of these was his inability to grasp an elemental understanding of public opinion and of national life.

If the National Front governments thought Rojas had the ability to appeal to the masses, they probably would have restricted him more carefully. In 1962, although they had taken away Rojas' political rights, they allowed him to declare himself for the presidency and to campaign. They afterwards were vindicated by his poor showing of only 2.1% of the votes. It seems clear that the growth of Anapo in the following years did not come from the general's personal charisma.

At best, Rojas provided a symbol. He was the only nonparty president—or even politician—that Colombia had had. He was a natural focal point for those who opposed the traditional parties, but he was hardly capable of molding a strong political movement.

As General Rojas grew older (70 in 1970) and weaker from diabetes (hospitalized after the elections), Anapo grew stronger. The leadership behind the scenes and the organizational force came from his daughter, Maria Eugenia Rojas de Moreno Diaz. Until the formal leadership of the Party was placed in her hands in 1971, she had always acted in her father's name. He had started her on a public career at the age of 21, when he had named her to head the newly established welfare agency, SENDAS. (Evita Peron had played a similar role in Argentina.) Maria Eugenia received continued public exposure as she visited hospitals, orphanages, and health centers, and distributed Christmas presents to children. She discribed herself in the final great rally in Bogota before the elections, in an article in *Alerta* on April 7, 1970:

> No one has known me in the past to be affiliated with one of the old parties or exercising sectarianism. I was known simply as a sincere woman, drying the tears of the widows of the violence, founding nurseries, covering the nakedness of the outcast youth, visiting the guerrillas in their jungle dens, looking for work for the unemployed, hospitals for the dying, and carrying the presents of the Christ Child to the children of the poor on Christmas Eve.

When the Anapo movement was initiated in 1962, Maria Eugenia was elected to Congress from Bogota. In 1966 and 1970, she was elected to the Senate. An article in a popular Colombian magazine (Flash, 1970) cited Maria Eugenia's occupation as: "Politician, she exercises it 18 hours a day, during seven days a week, thirty days a month, 365 days a year, for eight years of campaign." The article goes on:

> Maria Eugenia has a strong determined personality; she knows what she wants and where she is going. She is not afraid of anything, and her principal goal is to advance, advance. She has what the politicians call 'charisma,' which is something which maddens *(enloquece)* the masses and captivates those who talk personally with her. Her people consider her sacred, and many feel privileged if they can touch her. Nevertheless, Maria Eugenia is simple, her vocabularly is not refined, her consideration of national problems is straight forward.

She was called, "la Capitana del Pueblo," (Captain of the People), and held the formal position of campaign manager. Whereas the general was given the center of the stage at all important rallies and made the principal speeches, Maria Eugenia travelled more, spoke more, established the campaign strategy, and built the organization.

The program developed by Anapo is pragmatic and is not based on any coherent ideology. The only leader of Anapo capable of developing a coherent ideology, Hernando Olano Cruz, died prematurely of cancer in 1965 before he could leave any great imprint on the movement. In their principles, Anapo does not sound too different from the National Front. The leaders of Anapo, however, never cease to point out that the National Front is corrupt, made up of self-serving oligarchs, and has accomplished nothing of what it said it would. The most repeated point that is made is the comparison of the prosperity during the Rojas administration and the inflation and devaluations of the National Front period.

Another theme that appears in most speeches is that General Rojas stopped the war between the parties, and Anapo remains above the traditional party conflict. The parties are blamed for initiating the violence which began in the 1940s. The Anapo flag, a tricolor with white separating the blue and the red, symbolizes this point, and these flags are seen everywhere except in the upper-class barrios.

The Rojas campaign did come out with some definite policy proposals, though much of what was promised would require heavy expenditures, including education and welfare. Anapo claimed that these expenditures were possible without raising taxes because the party would eliminate the graft and waste of the National Front government. Rojas also promised to freeze prices, nationalize importations, stimulate exports, and revalue the peso to put it on a par with the dollar. The land reform of the National Front received a great amount of criticism, but Anapo did not plan to expropriate land either; rather it would distribute uncultivated and government land. Rojas said he would "respect capital" but proposed that workers should share in the profits.

It is very difficult to discover anything in the recorded statements about the Anapo program that would have attracted the poorest groups in such numbers and repelled the upper class: Rojas denounced the oligarchs, but even the traditional party leaders denounce the oligarchs in Colombia; Rojas denied that he wanted to divide the classes. Perhaps the poor believed Maria Eugenia (Rojas de Moreno Diaz, 1970) when she said:

I wish to win power for the purpose of undertaking a great work in benefit of the abandoned zones, since it is not justice that the rich *barrios* should have all the conveniences and the poor *barrios* should lack every service. I want the street lights to shine not only on the elegant zones but even on the forgotten and broken down shacks, where exist the most desolate scenes of hunger and misery. I want all the barrios to have water and sewers, that their streets should be passable, and that there be no more invalids nor that there be no more children sleeping in the entranceways covered with rags and papers in the cold and insupportable nights of the capital.

When the National Front made similar statements in more general language, they failed to win the votes from the poor.

Closely related to the question of program is the question of support from specific organized and unorganized groups in society. Peron had the labor unions, and it is doubtful that his movement could have been sustained without their support. As we stated, Rojas had no groups of loyal supporters when he left the presidency. In 1970, he had managed to win the support of only a few organized groups. For the most part, the organized workers remained loyal to the National Front, though some opted for Betancur rather than Pastrana. Only an occasional union resisted the labor confederations' pressure and endorsed Rojas. The only organized group that brought substantial support to the Rojas cause was the organization of military reservists, *Accion Patriotica Nacional (Patrianal)*. However, the movement may have been aided by unorganized groups of radicals.

The Anapo movement began as a Conservative splinter group and continued to maintain some of that character. Certain rural conservatives gave Rojas overwhelming support, and many of the older Anapo leaders around Rojas had been loyal Conservatives. Throughout the past ten years, Anapo has received defections from the Conservative Party leaders and has, in turn, lost some of its leaders to the official Conservative Party. On the most sensitive issue of Church-state relations, birth control, Anapo came out for the traditional Conservative position. Speaking for the Movement for a Vote of Conscience, a group organized to fight birth control, Herman Vergara Delgado (1970) said:

All four candidates have declared themselves Catholic with respect to general principles of Christian morality, but only General Rojas Pinilla has made a declaration sufficiently clear, conclusive and solemn in relation to the question of our Movement. In every human decision something is assured and something is risked. We decided to vote for General Rojas Pinilla because what his government would assure in respect to spiritual values is more, much more, than what it risks in temporal values.

Anapo used the birth control issue to attack the Liberals and show that "good Catholics" should not support the National Front.

Patrianal, the organization of retired military men, made a formal endorsement of Rojas in early March. Many of the ex-officers who belonged to this group had been retired from the military because of their support for Rojas. The organization proclaimed its support of Rojas because he was a military man who would bring about needed social changes. Also, he was the only candidate who

> pointed out the urgent need to structure a solid national defense on the base of a vigorous economy which would permit the renewal of material, equipment, and revenue of the Army, Navy, Air Force, and Police in order that the four forces can fulfill with pride their assigned mission, defending the foreign and domestic security of the fatherland.

Members of Patrianal were active in organizing and maintaining order at most Anapo rallies, and they turned out in force with a claimed 40,000 at a special rally in Bogota on March 6.

The leftist radicals in Colombia have no organized party to represent them, and Anapo tried to attract them with some success. The followers of Gaitan, some of the defunct MRL, a group of radical priests called Golconda, and the recent Liberal rebel José Ignacio (Nacho) Vives joined or gave qualified support for the Anapo movement.

When Rojas came to power in 1953, some of the followers of the assassinated Liberal leader, Jorge Eliécer Gaitan, joined his administration and have continued to work with him. In addition, Rojas used and continues to use many of the same populist themes developed by Gaitan. In 1969, Anapo was given the use of Gaitan's former headquarters in Bogota. In January 1970, the *Diario del Pueblo,* which claims to be the newspaper of *Gaitanismo* came out in support of Rojas because he "saved the Liberals from extinction" and was a middle-class person who opposed the oligarchy. The memory of Gaitan is still strong in Colombia, and the association that Anapo can make with Gaitanismo strengthens the party greatly among the nominal Liberals.

A minority of the MRL also went over to Anapo when the MRL rejoined the Liberal Party in 1967. Ciro Rios Nieto, an ex-director of MRL in Santander, became a leader in the Anapo movement in that region. Anapo has developed considerable support in what was previously one of the strongest MRL areas, the Department of Meta located in the Llanos.

Nacho Vives, the Liberal Senator from the Atlantic Coast who accused the Minister of Agriculture, Enrique Peñalosa, of corruption, became an active leader of Anapo after the government jailed him for alleged corruption and developed a much stronger marxist message than that of the mainline Anapo. After the elections, Nacho continued to be prominent in the Anapo movement, but was expelled when he tried to challenge the leadership in 1972.

The conservative Catholic hierarchy in Colombia has produced a group of rebel priests, who have also helped the Anapo cause. Golconda, as this group of priests calls itself, came together in November 1968 to support the memory of Camilo Torres, the martyred priest who had joined the guerrillas and been killed in January 1966. Though Golconda advocated abstention in the 1970 election, Anapo supported their cause whenever they were arrested. One of the leaders of the group, René Garcia, published a short column in *Alerta,* in which he proclaimed the revolutionary message of the gospels. One week before the elections, the Political Committee of Golconda made a declaration in *Alerta* of April 12, 1970, which gave a qualified endorsement of Anapo:

> We can not be unacquainted with the popular mass which surrounds Anapo. We respect this sector of the Colombian people.
>
> We will be with the popular masses for the exaction of the promises which Anapo makes. But we are going further. The only way to realize the popular aspirations is the radical change of the ruling system. Only the Revolution toward socialism is capable of giving effective reply to the Colombian people.

Golconda's attacks on the National Front paralleled that of Anapo and helped weaken the National Front candidates. After the elections, René Garcia was reported to have been arrested along with the principal Anapo leaders for advocating violence.

It is hard to say exactly who Anapo represents, or for what reasons, but as long as Anapo remains the opposition it is not forced to clarify its contradictory tendencies. Its support in the early 1960s came from Conservative and ex-military groups, but increasingly support has come from leftist radicals.

In the campaign for the 1970 elections, Anapo surprised most observers with its ability to turn out its followers at rallies, put up posters, carry voters to the polls, and sign up members. It seemed to have its organization working in every barrio and *vereda.* It pulled together an organization at least as effective as that of the traditional parties and which operated much better than in previous elections.

The formal structure of Anapo had at its top the *Jefatura Unica,* occupied by General Rojas, and the campaign manager, Maria Eugenia.

Below them was the *Comando Nacional,* composed of fourteen persons with strength in their respective regions. Further down the chain of command was the *Comando Departamental,* the *Comando Municipal,* and the feminine committee. At the bottom was the *pueblo,* who took out formal membership by buying a carnet for either two or five pesos (apparently depending on ability to pay). The command structure ran from top to bottom, with General Rojas promulgating all the lists of candidates. The Comando Nacional had the power to expel members from the movement and did so regularly. General Rojas has given the best description of the authority pattern of Anapo (in *Alerta* of May 20, 1970):

> This is a monolithic movement, with a reasoned discipline and an unquestionable hierarchy. Part of the force of Anapo rests in the discipline which the members have practiced and in their respect for their leaders (Jefes). We will continue functioning in such a way as we are convinced that our success is due in great part to the way the militants have accepted and executed the orders of the Chief, of the Campaign Director, and of the National Command.

The Anapo organization gave the party greater control from the center and greater work participation at the bottom than has been the case with the traditional parties. In both the Liberal and Conservative parties, the power has continued to rest with the regional leaders and the local *gamonales.* Anapo, on the other hand, can make decisions at the national level and have them carried out at the regional level. At the same time, Anapo has developed a formal membership, something which the traditional parties failed to do. The membership is composed of volunteers and not just of government employees. There are no data on how successful the selling of membership cards nationally was, but in Valle, the organization claimed to have sold 150,000 carnets.

Anapo leaders come from a quite different sector of the population than do the leaders of the traditional parties. The Valle organizer and Senator for Anapo, Marco Fidel Rueda Portes, was a mechanic before becoming a full-time worker for Anapo. The description of Anapo representatives given by Richard Eder (1964) still fits:

> The Rojistas, short, swarthy men in ill fitting suits, have introduced a violent note into the Congress session.
>
> 'Why some of these people are known criminals,' one Liberal Congressman said as the Rojistas shouted, booed and all but drowned out President Valencia's attempt to open Congress last week.

Whether they are criminals or not must be decided by a court of law, but the Liberal Congressman's perception dramatizes the way the traditional upper-class politicians view the more disreputable representatives of Anapo.

This description of Anapo gives some hint as to the source of its strength, especially with the lower class. It has organization made up of middle-class persons who have gone out and organized the masses. They are led by a woman who holds the confidence of the masses when she says that she wants to do something for them. The most uncertain aspect of the movement is its relationship with the leftist radicals. The left has little prominence in the formal organization, which is still tightly controlled by the original leaders of the movement. It is not known how close the left is to Maria Eugenia personally, nor how important leftist views are for the voting masses. Only the future can say how these different and contradictory elements will fit together or fail to fit together.

THE CAMPAIGN

Campaigning was intense in 1970. The classic pattern, where the presidential candidate travels to every major town of the country with the local leaders bringing out the citizens to attend large rallies and hear everybody's speeches is still the pattern most used by the political leaders. The newspapers, fulfilling a very important role, especially in informing the local leaders, belong to national and regional political figures, and they support the candidate of their faction both in editorials and news reporting, which is almost never unbiased.

New media are being used to supplement the old forms. Radio transmitters are more numerous than newspapers, and there are some independent networks. Anapo operated a national transmitter for the four months before the election. Television is owned by the government, and each of the four candidates was given the opportunity to address the nation, but television sets are not yet available to the lower classes.

In Colombia, the persons holding administrative positions in the government are not supposed to campaign. The *Procurador General* is responsible for enforcing this regulation. For the most part, the rule was followed in 1970, and the persons who carried out the National Front campaign had all resigned from their positions in the previous year. In the last few weeks of the campaign, however, President Lleras felt compelled to go to the people to defend his administration's policies. In the course of his defense, he attacked Rojas, and the Procurador General submitted his resignation in protest. Though the resignation was refused, the point was made.

The major campaign efforts for the National Front were made by the candidate himself, Misael Pastrana, and the second most important Liberal politician, Julio Cesar Turbay. Turbay was officially the *designado,* the person without administrative position who takes over for the president when he is out of the country or incapacitated. Together, the two campaigned in all parts of the country, as did General Rojas and Maria Eugenia. The strength of the Rojas entourage was shown very early by the far larger crowds attending its rallies in major cities. These were not, of course, spontaneous crowds, but were the result of careful organizational work and in many cases required the provision of transportation.

Newspaper coverage was almost exclusively favorable to Pastrana. Sourdis had support from one Conservative chain, owned by Alvaro Caicedo, and from Atlantic Coast newspapers. Betancur had limited support, but was able to get fairly objective coverage from all the newspapers. The major newspapers treated Rojas as if he did not exist except when President Lleras attacked him. They also refused to carry Anapo advertising, and when the second most import Liberal newspaper, *El Expectador,* published a paid advertisement for Anapo, it was roundly rebuked by the other papers. Since it was impossible to learn anything about Anapo from reading the major press, the movement started publishing its own newspaper, *Alerta,* toward the end of 1969, but it had very limited readership.

Regional leaders are usually very active during the campaign period, as they are often candidates for some representative office, whether senator, representative, deputy, or councilman. For the first time in Colombia, the election for these representative offices came at the same time as the presidential elections. Therefore, the lists were designated as being Liberal or Conservative in favor of Pastrana, Rojas, Betancur, or Sourdis. Regional leaders travelled nearly every day to some part of their departments to drink *aguardiente* with the local leaders and address the assembled followers of the faction, gathering support for the presidential candidates along with their own.

The preelectoral survey sought information on which of those who intended to vote for president had read about candidates, which had listened to speeches of candidates, and how many had attended rallies. Table 8 gives the results by area and candidate. Since Sourdis had no active campaign in Valle, his few voters are not included in the results. The biggest difference between the voters for the different candidates appears in the attendance at rallies. Rojas organizers clearly brought the electorate

TABLE 8
CAMPAIGN RESPONSE (percentage of voters for candidate)

	Pastrana	Rojas	Betancur
Have you read about candidates?			
Cali	73.6	61.3	65.5
Towns	68.3	56.6	75.0
Rural	64.3	57.0	62.1
Have you listened to speeches of candidates?			
Cali	74.5	66.9	77.4
Towns	70.4	63.2	90.0
Rural	72.3	74.8	79.3
Have you attended rallies of candidates?			
Cali	13.8[a]	31.5	31.0
Towns	40.7	45.1	42.5
Rural	24.1	43.9	31.0

a. Five Pastrana voters had attended only Rojas rallies.

out to mass rallies better than did Pastrana organizers, particularly in Cali and the rural area. In the towns, the Pastrana organizers did almost as well as the Rojas organizers.

A somewhat smaller proportion of Rojas voters than Pastrana voters had read about the candidates. What they read must have been largely against Rojas and for Pastrana, but apparently this did not bother them. The rural voters read almost as much as did the urban and town voters, but this result should not be considered representative of all rural residents, because the interviewed rural voters all lived fairly close to towns. A slightly higher proportion of voters had listened to candidates' speeches than had read about candidates, which would be possible only in a society where the radio is the predominate means of communication. More than

TABLE 9
BEST MEANS OF INFORMATION[a] (in percentages)

	Cali	Towns	Rural	Pastrana	Rojas	Betancur	Sourdis	All
Flyers and posters	.9	2.6	.0	1.3	1.5	0	0	1.2
Radio	63.6	61.3	81.7	60.7	72.2	69.1	43.7	66.1
Newspapers	22.7	23.0	9.9	25.8	15.5	16.3	25.0	20.4
Television	9.9	4.7	1.5	8.0	4.9	9.8	18.7	7.1
Public meetings and talks with politicians	1.1	3.3	2.0	1.1	2.5	2.4	0	1.9
Conversation with friends	1.4	3.7	2.5	1.9	2.5	1.6	6.2	2.2
Other	.4	1.4	2.5	1.1	.8	.8	6.2	1.1
Total	100	100	100	100	100	100	100	100
n	(632)	(300)	(202)	(524)	(471)	(123)	(16)	(1,134)

a. By location and by presidential preference.

two-thirds of the voters interviewed in Valle claimed to have listened to the speeches of at least one of the candidates, and 85% of listeners had listened to more than one candidate.

The survey also asked which media the voter had used to inform himself and, of those, which he had considered to be the best. Table 9 gives the results by area. Ten percent more of the Rojas voters than Pastrana voters thought radio was the best medium, while the reverse was true for newspapers. For all voters, radio was chosen as the best medium by over 60%, and newspapers by 20%. Television lagged a distant third with 7%. What is most striking about the results on this question is that rallies, talks with politicians, and conversation with friends are almost never (5%) considered the best medium. Voters consistently chose the newer forms of communication over the traditional ones.

Level of Information

The preelectoral Valle study also attempted to assess the information level of the interviewees by asking them to name persons in important political positions and the presidential candidates. Table 10 gives the percentage of correct answers. The population is not badly informed when one considers the average level of education. The large number of persons who could name all four presidential candidates (79.8%) indicates the high

TABLE 10
SCORES ON POLITICAL INFORMATION

Pastrana	Rojas	Betancur	Nonvotees
6.46 (621)[a]	5.57 (530)	6.70 (150)	5.23 (623)
Cali	**Town**	**Rural**	
6.06 (1,168)	5.86 (487)	4.91 (403)	
Radio	**Newspapers**	**TV**	**Conversations**
5.66 (1,140)	6.38 (314)	6.70 (124)	5.33 (46)

All differences significant at .05 level except differences between conversations and radio.

	Percentage Correct Answers on Separate Questions	
President (Lleras)	92.6	(1,997)
All four presidential candidates	79.8	(1,973)
Mayor of municipio	60.8	(2,003)
One senator from department of Valle	23.8	(1,995)
Minister of Foreign Relations (Lopez)	21.9	(1,973)
One deputy from department of Valle	9.7	(1,981)
Minister of Agriculture (Samper)	5.2	(1,990)

a. Parentheses contain n's.

level of attention given to the presidential campaign, especially since Sourdis did not campaign and was unknown in Valle before the campaign. Even 72.1% of those who did not plan to vote could name all four presidential candidates.

The comparison of mean levels of information between different groups shows how levels of information vary throughout Valle. The variation is not great, with the standard deviation for all groups being below 2.0 and the differences between means not exceeding 1.2. The Rojas voters had only a slightly higher level of information than the nonvoters. The Pastrana and Betancur voters were quite a bit higher. Those that considered radio the best means of communication were less well informed than those that relied more on newspapers and television. The difference, however, may be due either to education or location of residence rather than the media. The rural and the less educated were more likely to consider the radio the best means of communication, and they also have lower levels of information.

Did the Campaign Change your Opinion?

The campaign did change some opinions, according to the Valle data. We have two types of evidence for this assertion: The open question on both the pre- and postelectoral surveys, and the comparison of pre- and postelectoral choice for president by class.

Table 11 shows that those who recorded having changed their opinion are male rather than female, young rather than old (21-30), and the more educated rather than less educated. (University educated = 19.3%, a very high percentage relative to the other categories.) The young feel less affiliated with the parties than the older population, which may explain why the campaign would influence their vote.

A comparison of pre- and postelectoral preference in Cali divided by

TABLE 11
DID THE CAMPAIGN CHANGE YOUR OPINION?
(postelectoral, Cali)

Age	Male	Female	Education	
21-25	14.6	7.1	0	4.2
26-30	16.3	6.6	1, 2P	5.5
31-40	7.7	5.4	3-5P	5.5
41-50	4.1	7.3	1-3S	7.4
51-60	4.4	1.8	4-6S	11.7
More than 60	8.9	6.7	Univ.	19.3
Total	7.8	5.9	Total	6.9 (n=1,207)

TABLE 12
COMPARISON BETWEEN PRE AND POST STUDIES BY
CLASS, CALI, VOTE SHIFT BETWEEN
CANDIDATES (in percentages)

	Pastrana	Rojas	Betancur
Upper	+9.1	−4.6	−5.3
Middle	+7.1	−11.7	+3.6
Working	+9.9	−8.1	+.1
Lower	−8.0	+12.4	−4.4

class on Table 12 indicates a definite deepening of the class division between the National Front candidates and the Anapo candidate. This shift took place in the very last days of the campaign (the Cali preelectoral survey was finished on Thursday before elections). Pastrana gained upper-class votes from Rojas and Betancur; middle- and working-class votes from Rojas; Rojas picked up lower-class votes from both Pastrana and Betancur.

Effects of the Campaign: Motivations to Vote

Two sections were included in the Valle study which dealt specifically with the reasons felt or expressed by the voters in choosing to vote for a candidate: first, a series of reasons which might have been important, where the voter expressed agreement or disagreement about the importance of the specific reason; second, an open question where the interviewee could express his principal reason for voting for his candidate.

The responses to the closed question are summarized on Table 13 rather than given for each candidate, because there was general agreement among the supporters of different candidates. Rojas voters scored slightly higher on importance of speaking ability, and Pastrana voters scored

TABLE 13
REASONS FOR PRESIDENTIAL CHOICE
(preelectoral; in percentages)

	Yes	No	Don't Know
Was the following important in your decision of whom to vote for?			
Candidate's program	91.9	5.4	2.7
Candidate's personality	84.8	12.7	2.5
Party's program	80.5	16.2	3.3
Candidate's speaking ability	65.8	28.6	5.6
Opinion of national political leaders	53.0	41.5	5.5
Opinion of local political leaders	45.0	49.6	5.4
Candidate's regional base	21.8	76.0	2.2

somewhat higher on importance of the opinion of national political leaders. Otherwise, the different groups of voters varied no more than a few percentage points.

Program was chosen as "important" by the largest percentage of voters on the closed questions and was named as "most important" by 53.5% of the voters, as is seen on Table 14. An important conclusion to be drawn from these data is the fact that the "personalist" factor or "conditions" played a role of minor importance as a motivating force for the electorate in 1970 (especially for voters for the two major contenders).

Another factor which was apparently felt to be of little importance for most of the electorate was party discipline (importance given to national or local leaders). The Pastrana voters registered a larger percentage than the others on this factor, but even for them, it was weak. The "regional origin" of the candidate was of least importance in a department without native son candidates, but was important, judging from the official results, in areas with native son candidates. Sourdis won the majority of votes in the Atlantic region, Betancur came close to winning in Caldas, and Pastrana received his strongest majority in Huila.

According to the data we do have, program is the most important reason for voting for all groups.

To illustrate this conclusion, we have included examples of the answers given to the open question "why did you vote for X?" It is clear that the category "program" (very generally understood) is the most typical type:

Most typical Anapistas responses: "He is the candidate of the poor." "He is with the People." "I trust that his government would change the conditions of the poor." "Because he understands the situation." "Because he will take care of the situation." "Because I don't agree with this

TABLE 14
MOST IMPORTANT REASON FOR PRESIDENTIAL
CHOICE (preelectoral; in percentages) (n = 1,450)

	Pastrana	Rojas	Belisario	Sourdis	Undecided	Total
Candidate's party	6.7	5.2	5.3	10.5	9.2	6.2
The least bad	0.6	0.2	1.3	0.0	0.0	.4
Candidate's personality	14.3	12.5	17.2	31.6	3.7	13.8
Program of candidate or party	50.6	61.7	53.0	26.3	35.8	53.5
Opinions of local or national leaders	8.0	2.0	0.0	0.0	0.9	4.2
Other	11.8	10.7	11.9	10.5	8.2	11.1
Don't know	8.0	7.7	11.3	21.1	42.2	10.9
Total	100.0	100.0	100.0	100.0	100.0	100.0

[Lleras'] government." "Because Rojas is with the poor. Perhaps, he can educate the children." "Because he respects the popular class. He opposes the oligarchy." "In order to organize the country with justice." "He is in the opposition." "The others have not fulfilled their promises." "He is going to help the people." "Rojas—for the economic conditions of the unemployed." "Rojas—we want a change." "He has been the President of the poor." "I am bored with the others and I want to put a brake on the high price of living." "He did works which have not been surpassed by the National Front." "For impulses that seize one at times." "To pull down the hegemony which goes against esthetics."

Most typical Pastranistas responses: "He is the official candidate." "He is the candidate of the National Front." "I vote for Pastrana for peace and progress." "He is the candidate of my party [Liberal]." "To support his policy." "The candidate who offers me the most guarantees." "In order to continue the work of Lleras." "The others don't work and promise much." "He is a good Conservative and has a good program." "He has the best ideas and my friends advised me to vote for him." "He is the best prepared to manage the country." "I vote for the National Front because it has brought a line of progress to the country." "With Pastrana there will be more peace and security." "He seems to me to be better, the most able." "He has the program of the National Front." "In order that the country does not fall into a civil war." "He is the man accepted by the National Liberal Directorate and dissidence is not good." "In order to benefit the people." "Because it is the force of the main stream." "One will see that he can be a good President." "In order to continue the National Front." "Because the others are pure straw [paja]."

Typical Belisaristas answers: "He is with the people." "He is well prepared." "He has a good program." "He is with the worker." "He can be a good president." "Against the imposed candidate."

REASONS FOR NOT VOTING

The Valle preelectoral survey examined the reasons for not voting in the same way that it examined the reasons for choosing a particular candidate. In the first open question, 33.3% of the nonvoters gave responses that were classified as lack of interest. Some typical ones are: "I don't have time to leave the house—in any case everything will continue badly." "I am not interested." "I have no special reason." "I don't understand politics."

TABLE 15
REASON FOR NOT VOTING (preelectoral; in percentages)

	Yes	No	Don't Know	Total
Unhappy with candidates	72.9	20.8	7.1	100
Uninterested in politics	71.2	25.6	3.2	100
Insufficient information	53.8	39.6	6.6	100
Vote lacks importance	34.6	54.2	11.2	100
Discontent with the situation	23.6	70.5	5.9	100
Satisfied with the situation	23.6	67.9	6.5	100
Candidate came from other department	11.2	81.1	7.7	100

The first response indicates that lack of interest does not always reflect satisfaction with the situation. When asked specifically whether lack of interest was important or not, 71.2% said it was important, but only 23.6% said that satisfaction with the situation was important (Table 15). Only 1.1% said that being satisfied was the most important reasons for not voting (Table 16).

A large number of respondents gave answers that indicated that their reason for not voting related to their dissatisfaction with the political system, the general situation, or with the candidates. In response to the first open question, 17.5% gave answers that indicated they were discontent with the system and 23.2% voiced disapproval of the candidates. Some typical answers were: "All elections are frauds." "Because they are very demogogic." "There is no truth in their promises." "I don't agree with the system." "Because whoever comes to power will just strangle the people more." "I am not voting for President because I am not satisfied with any candidate." "Because the parties are united." "As an old man, I have no right to work; therefore why should I help." "Because the four candidates are conservative." "Because the candidates

TABLE 16
MOST IMPORTANT REASON FOR NOT VOTING
(preelectoral; in percentages)

	Cali	Towns	Rural	Total
Satisfied	1.7	0	0	1.1
Discontent	29.7	19.6	12.3	24.7
Vote has no importance	1.9	1.0	.7	1.5
Lack of interest	40.0	42.3	50.8	42.5
Only Conservative candidates	6.3	15.5	6.9	7.8
Other	15.3	10.3	17.7	15.0
Don't know	5.1	11.3	11.6	7.4
Total	100	100	100	100
n	(413)	(97)	(130)	(640)

don't fulfill their promises." The discontent with the political and economic situations seemed to weigh less heavily than a distaste for the particular candidates or politicians in general. Asked whether only having Conservative candidates to vote for was important, 72.9% said that it was, but only 7.8% said it was the most important reason. When asked if discontent with the situation was important, 34.6% said yes. An understanding of the nature of this discontent will become clearer when the opinions and attitudes of voters and nonvoters are compared in a later section.

Women were much more likely to give lack of interest as the most important reason for not voting than were men (40% versus 28%), and the men expressed much more discontent with the system (21% versus 13%) and the candidates (29% versus 17%). Among the classes in Cali, the middle class was most likely to give discontent with the system as the main reason for not voting; the working class, discontent with the candidates; and the lower class, lack of interest. The age group that was most likely to give discontent with both the system and the candidates was between 50 and 60 years of age.

COLOMBIAN REGIONAL VOTING PATTERNS

In order to fully understand why the 1970 election turned out the way it did, it would be necessary to study carefully every village and barrio in Colombia. Each area has its own pattern of politics depending upon the personal and social characteristics of the area. The variety of these characteristics is enormous. The complete returns by municipio of the 1970 elections have not yet been published, but we do have returns from each of the departments and for many of the cities. This section will deal with these larger patterns.

Table 17 presents the simple correlations of some social and political variables and three different voting statistics by department. For the most

TABLE 17
CORRELATIONS OF DEPARTMENTAL VOTING

Variables	Pastrana Vote	Rojas Vote	% Voting
Literacy	−.21	.42	−.12
Percentage born in department	.31	−.36	.10
Agricultural employment	.44	−.17	−.30
Land tenancy	−.10	.65	−.20
Vote for MRL in 1962	−.27	.45	.03
Vote for Gaitan in 1946	−.40	−.36	.36

part, the correlations are not high. Since each department contains many life-style variations—such as urban-rural, poor-rich—it should not be expected that any correlations by department could be high.

Generally, the Pastrana vote was highest in the less-developed areas, where literacy was low, most of the residents had lived in the department all their life, and agricultural employment was high. He did not do well where the MRL had done well in 1962, nor where Gaitan had done well in 1946.

On the other hand, Rojas did well where literacy was higher, where fewer were born in the department where they lived, where MRL had done well, and where there was a high proportion of land tenancy by renting and tenant farming. But he did not do well where Gaitan had had the highest vote—i.e., the Atlantic Coast—where Sourdis did best.

The patterns become much more apparent when the major regions of Colombia are discussed separately. Dividing Colombia into five regions oversimplifies even more than does dividing it into departments, but it does highlight some more factors as well as allowing us to point out the exceptions and special cases.

The Atlantic region has always felt itself to be quite separated from the central part of Colombia, a fact which saved it from most of the rural violence that racked the rest of Colombia. The area has been going through a new period of growth in recent years as Barranquilla has expanded industrially and cotton and palm oil production has increased. On the other hand, the regional politicians make much of the fact that the area has been slighted in government services and investments. Public services in the cities, education, and transportation have lagged. The region has always had a strong Liberal majority. Gaitan was strongest here in 1946, and the MRL did well in 1962.

The region went strongly for Sourdis in the 1970 election (Table 18). He was the regional candidate and campaigned on the program of helping the neglected areas. This Sourdis vote had an element of protest in it, but it did not go so far as rejecting the National Front and the traditional parties. The percentage of population voting held up very well. Pastrana did well only in the more rural and less developed departments of Sucre and Cordoba. Rojas ran ahead of Pastrana in three of the region's six departments, doing best in the city of Santa Marta where he gained 60% of the vote. José Jaramillo, the Liberal Anapo candidate for president in 1966, had done fairly well in the area. The Anapo vote made smaller gains here in 1970 than it did in most other parts of the country.

As one moves inland along the Eastern Cordillera and to the Llanos or plains one comes to the strongest Anapo area. This area, containing some

TABLE 18
ELECTION RESULTS BY DEPARTMENTS

Department	Pastrana %	Rojas %	Betancur %	Sourdis %	Voters n	Voting %
Atlantic Coast						
More developed						
Magdalena	26.6	31.3	1.2	40.8	124,096	48
Atlantica	16.3	31.5	1.3	50.8	200,211	52
Bolivar	28.1	26.6	2.8	42.5	157,483	48
Less developed						
Guajira	30.3	35.3	1.8	32.5	46,630	53
Sucre	43.8	21.3	.7	34.1	83,052	48
Cordoba	46.3	36.3	4.3	13.2	136,691	49
Urbanized						
More developed						
Antioquia	41.7	41.9	16.0	,0.4	457,397	38
Cundinamarca	42.8	42.4	13.8	,1.0	775,744	51
Valle	38.9	48.0	12.1	1.0	405,787	46
Extractive						
High tenancy						
Cesar	21.0	45.1	0.9	33.1	71,249	38
Norte de Santander	47.1	44.1	,8.4	0.3	135,674	57
Santander	36.5	52.2	10.6	0.9	242,452	54
Boyacá	36.1	55.8	7.7	0.3	198,148	42
Meta	31.7	50.5	17.6	0.3	45,177	39
Central						
More developed						
Caldas	38.6	29.3	31.9	0.2	138,735	46
Risaralda	46.0	31.3	22.5	0.2	89,945	44
Quindio	40.4	35.9	23.4	0.2	58,698	32
Southwest						
Less developed						
Tolima	47.2	39.8	12.8	0.1	156,908	45
Huila	63.9	26.1	,9.9	.0	105,987	55
Cauca	59.1	22.4	18.4	0.2	119,112	38
Chocó	52.4	10.8	35.6	1.1	36,403	46
Nariño	56.7	23.1	12.3	7.9	151,878	42

of the oldest settlments in Colombia, is where the violence began in the 1940s. It is not particularly well developed, and the population is less literate than in the more advanced areas. The largely traditional agriculture has been penetrated by the extractive industries of petroleum, iron, and steel. Although these industries do not provide a high amount of employment, they have brought with them some radical organized labor.

Rojas received over 50% of the vote in Santander, Boyacá, and Meta. Santander and Meta had had Liberal majorities and had been the strongest MRL centers in the country. On the other hand, Boyacá had been one of the strongest Conservative departments and had given very little support to the MRL. Cesar, which has only recently been separated from Magdalena, was also a strong Liberal and MRL area.

Antioquia, Cundinamarca, and Valle contain the three major cities of Colombia, along with some of the most prosperous commercial agriculture. The departments have also been favored with government development projects. The major cities have long had Liberal majorities, but the MRL had done well only in Valle.

The three major cities, Medillin, Bogota, and Cali all gave pluralities to Rojas. Pastrana did much better in Cundinamarca outside Bogota. Rojas did well in Antioquia and Valle outside the cities, and even better in rural Valle than he did in Cali. The Sourdis vote is totally unimportant here, but Betancur did relatively well.

The prosperous coffee area of Caldas, Risaralda, and Quindio had its own pattern of politics. Most farmers own their own property here, and literacy tends to be high. The area is traditionally Conservative. Betancur ran more strongly here than in any other part of Colombia, but Pastrana still held the pluralities. Rojas was no stronger here than he was in the Atlantic Coast.

The southwest region has a great deal of variation, but it is generally more rural than most of the rest of the country, and the land is relatively well distributed. Huila and Tolima have prosperous coffee areas, but there are few other commercial crops. Huila, Tolima, and Cauca experienced considerable violence, but Nariño and Chocó were not touched. Cauca, Huila, and Tolima have had Liberal majorities and a high MRL vote. Nariño has been Conservative, with no MRL. Chocó, the most underdeveloped department in Colombia, has a strong Liberal vote, but also no MRL.

Pastrana comes from Huila, and he received his highest total there— 63.9% of the vote. He ran more strongly throughout the whole area than he did elsewhere in Colombia, and Rojas ran more weakly in the region, except in Tolima, than in any other part of the country.

The association of certain characteristics at the department level does not, of course, indicate why some people voted for one candidate and others voted for another. Whereas Anapo did well in the MRL areas of Cesar, Santander, and Meta, it is not at all clear that Rojas received votes from those who had previously been active in the MRL. From other sources, we know he received some support from them, but we do not know how much. Much of the rural Anapo vote has come from Conservatives, whom the MRL opposed. Nor is it at all clear why the areas with the highest amount of tenant farming should be strong Anapo areas. Rojas' stand on land reform was even more equivocal than that of the National Front.

One of the important questions for the future of Anapo is the extent to which it was able to capture Liberal votes. In areas where Anapo ran separate Liberal and Conservative congressional lists, it is possible to assess its relative pull with the two traditional constituencies. In two strong Liberal areas, Santander and Antioquia, Anapo received as many votes on its Conservative lists as it did on its Liberal ones. In Cundinamarca and Valle, Anapo's Conservative lists did about twice as well as its Liberal lists. On this very critical question, then, the 1970 results were ambiguous. In some areas the Anapo Liberals have done very well, but in others they have been weak.

PRESIDENTIAL VOTE AND SOCIOECONOMIC CATEGORIES

The most significant aspect of the 1970 election was the development of class voting in Colombia. The evidence is clear from the official data published by DANE on voting in Medellin and Bogota. It comes out clearly in the Los Andes survey of voters in Bogota and our surveys in the Departmento del Valle. Before discussing the results for presidential vote, we will discuss who voted and who did not in 1970 and compare them with the voters in the congressional elections of 1968.

In 1970, as in 1968, those with less education, the poor, the young, and female all voted less than their opposites. This tendency has been noted in other countries, and may well be a universal phenomenon. A comparison of the 1968 with the 1970 results shows that the degree of abstention by these groups may vary considerably. We find that with the exception of the male-female difference, the difference in voting percentage between the categories is sharply reduced in 1970. Many more voted in 1970 than in 1968, although those surveyed both years reported an intention to vote that was higher than the actual vote. The lower class, however, increased its vote far more than did the other classes (Table 19). In 1968, the middle class voted at a rate 40% higher than the lower class's. In 1970, this difference was reduced to 6%. The lower class also reported a higher intention to vote than did the working class; it was the lower classes that voted for Rojas. The Anapo campaign was able to mobilize groups of the population who in the past had not voted or had voted less.

More information on this issue was obtained by a question in the 1970 survey. We asked whether the interviewees had voted before and why not and compared this with their voting intentions in 1970 (Table 20). Only 75% of the Rojas voters had voted before, as compared to 95% of the Pastrana voters. Most of the new Rojas voters said that they had not voted

TABLE 19
CLASSES AND VOTING, 1968 AND 1970 (in percentages)

Class	Voting 1968 Congress	Voting 1970 President
Upper	50	87
Middle	44	66
Working	34	57
Lower	31	62

TABLE 20
VOTING PREFERENCES AND VOTES IN THE PAST
(preelectoral; in percentages)

Presidential Preference	Voted Before	Not Voting Before				Total	n
		Discont. w/System	Lack of Interest	Lack of Age	Physical Obstacle		
Pastrana	94.8	0	1.2	3.5	0.5	100	(582)
Rojas	74.4	1.5	14.4	7.9	1.9	100	(533)
Betancur	84.3	0	8.5	6.5	0.7	100	(153)
Sourdis	78.9	5.3	10.5	5.3	0	100	(19)
Not voting for president	80.7	7.6	7.6	3.8	0	100	(26)
Nonvoters	55.1	3.4	31.6	8.6	1.3	100	(610)
Undecided	86.7	0.9	10.5	1.9	0	100	(105)
Total	75.8	1.6	15.0	6.4	1.1	100	(2,028)

TABLE 21
VOTING AND AGE (in percentages)

Age	Voting Preelectoral	1970 Postelectoral	Voting 1968
21-25	58.0	38.6	26
25-30	61.6	53.2	26
31-40	67.0	65.4	33
41-50	72.6	69.8	44
51-60	69.3	69.6	51
60 plus	71.1	56.7	51

TABLE 22
AGE AND PRESIDENTIAL VOTE (preelectoral; in percentages)

Age	Pastrana	Rojas	Betancur	Total	n
21-30	40.8	49.5	9.7	100	(299)
31-40	45.1	41.9	13.0	100	(408)
41-50	49.5	36.5	14.0	100	(321)
51-60	51.8	41.8	7.1	100	(170)
60 plus	58.8	29.4	8.5	100	(102)
Total	47.2	41.2	11.6	100	(1,300)

$X^2 = 23.499$ (significant at .005)

before because of lack of interest. From the same table, one can see that 55% of those who were abstaining in 1970 had voted before. The choice available in 1970, while it had aroused many new voters, had also failed to interest many others who previously had found the vote meaningful.

In addition to the lower-class vote, Rojas also brought out the younger vote. Table 21 shows that the vote of the under-30 group jumped from 26% in 1968 to 60% in 1970. (The actual number would be less in both years). The young were still not voting to the same extent as the old, but the difference between them had appreciably narrowed. Looking back at Table 20, we see that those who were too young to have voted previously indicated a strong preference for Rojas. In the postelectoral survey, the group 25 and under reported a lower proportion voting than was anticipated in the preelectoral survey. The difference was accounted for by those, especially women, who did not have the *cedulas* required for voting.

In our sample in the Department of Valle de Cauca, we found that age was a statistically significant [at the .005 level] explanation of presidential voting (Table 22). The survey conducted in Bogota by the *Universidad de los Andes* (1970) did not find a statistically significant relationship. There was an agreement in the two studies on the tendency of the younger voters to vote for Rojas but the tendency was stronger in Valle.

The 1970 preelectoral survey also showed that those who have lived in their present municipio only a short time vote less than others. This had not been examined in 1968. Table 23 shows that those who have lived in Cali less than one year, from one to three years, and from five to fifteen years are less likely to vote than are the other groups. The persons who have lived in their present municipio from five to fifteen years moved during the period of intense rural violence and appear to behave differently from those who migrated during the more peaceful recent period. Those who have lived less than one year in the municipio tend to have more problems with the cedula than the other groups.

The migrants that tended to abstain more also tended to have a higher vote for Rojas, indicating again that Rojas was able to mobilize some of the groups with a high abstention rate. A majority of those who voted and lived less than one year in the municipio stated that they would vote for Rojas (Table 24). The second-highest Rojas vote came from the group that migrated during the violence. Both of these groups also voted more than average for Betancur. Abstention, votes for Rojas, and votes for Betancur means that these are clearly nonconformist groups in the population in the Valle de Cauca.

The Universidad de los Andes survey of Bogota found that length of residence was not statistically significant in the Presidential vote, but that

TABLE 23
RESIDENCE IN MUNICIPIO (preelectoral)

	% Voting
Less than 1 year	60.2
1-3 years	63.9
3-5 years	72.5
5-15 years	63.1
15 years-all of life	67.4
All of life	70.7

TABLE 24
RESIDENCE IN MUNICIPIO AND PRESIDENTIAL VOTE
(preelectoral; in percentages)

Number of Years	Pastrana	Rojas	Betancur	Total	n
Less than 1 year	35.7	51.8	12.5	100	(56)
1-3 years	43.5	44.9	11.6	100	(69)
3-5 years	45.5	43.9	10.6	100	(66)
5-15 years	38.9	47.7	13.4	100	(350)
15 years—all of life	52.4	36.5	11.1	100	(370)
All of life	52.8	36.6	10.6	100	(407)
Total	47.4	41.0	11.6	100	(1,318)

X^2 = 22.932 (significant at .05 level)

TABLE 25
1968 ELECTIONS, BY CLASS, CALI (in percentages)

Class	Anapo	Conservative Lists	Liberal Lists	Total	n
Upper	0	27	73	100	(45)
Middle	12	21	67	100	(132)
Working	8	24	68	100	(58)
Lower	14	16	70	100	(108)

X^2 = 9.185 (not significant at .05 level)

TABLE 26
PREELECTORAL, CALI, INTENTION TO VOTE
(in percentages)

Class	Pastrana	Rojas	Betancur	Total	n
Upper	80.0	4.6	15.4	100	(65)
Middle	53.7	31.7	14.6	100	(82)
Working	44.8	43.4	11.8	100	(203)
Lower	38.5	50.8	10.7	100	(364)

X^2 = 53.937 (significant at .05 level)

place of birth was. The los Andes study showed that those who were born in towns of under 20,000 had a much greater tendency to vote for Rojas. The question in our survey was worded differently, but we found little difference in presidential candidate preference between those who came from rural areas and those who came from urban areas. It may be that the difference is in the nature of the locality from which Cali migrants came. These comparisons show that it is invalid to credit all urban migrants with similar behavior patterns, which depend on the circumstances under which they came to the urban areas and where they came from.

As in the los Andes study, we found that women and men voted very similarly. A few more men than women declared that they would vote for Rojas, but the difference was not large enough to be statistically significant. On the other hand, considerably more women than men said that they would not vote. Women formed the one group of abstainers that Anapo failed to mobilize.

A number of indicaters reflect socioeconomic stratification, and they all show the same thing: *Colombia in 1970 was polarized between those who had very little and those who had more.* The information from previous years is such that it is difficult to establish precisely the degree of class voting in earlier years. For 1970, on the other hand, we have evidence from the los Andes study, from the Universidad del Valle studies, and for vote by barrio in Medellin and Bogota.

The 1968 election survey in Cali (Table 25) did not reveal a class vote that was statistically significant. The traditional parties still dominated the scene, and they were multiclass parties. The Liberal lists received very close to the same proportion in every class, but the Conservative vote fell off among the lower class. Anapo received no upper-class votes, but it was almost as strong in the middle class as in the lower class.

The 1970 preelectoral survey (Table 26) shows that one week before the April elections that the situation had polarized. The percentage in the upper-class voting for Pastrana was twice as great as the percentage of the lower-class voting for Pastrana. The Rojas vote was even more stratified. When the same barrios were interviewed three weeks after the elections, the polarization appeared even greater (Table 27). Because of the similarities in sampling and in answers to other questions, we interpret this as being a real shift in voting behavior. The percentage of the upper class voting for Pastrana became three times as great as the percentage of the lower class voting for him. No upper-class respondents said they voted for Rojas, while 63% of the lower class vote went to him.

The class voting found in the postelectoral survey in Cali is very close to those found in the official results from stratified barrios in Bogota and

TABLE 27
POSTELECTORAL CALI

Class	Pastrana	Rojas	Betancur	Total	n
Upper	89.1	0	10.1	100	(64)
Middle	61.8	20.0	18.2	100	(110)
Working	52.7	35.3	11.9	100	(201)
Lower	30.5	63.2	6.3	100	(351)

$X^2 = 141.0008$ (significant at .05 level)

TABLE 28
OFFICIAL RESULTS IN STRATIFIED BARRIOS, BOGOTA
AND MEDELLIN (in percentages)

Class	Pastrana	Rojas	Betancur	Sourdis	Blancos	Total	n
Bogota							
Upper	75.8	8.3	11.9	3.5	.4	100	(21,499)
Upper-middle	67.0	11.9	17.6	3.0	.5	100	(22,668)
Middle	56.4	19.5	20.9	2.4	.8	100	(61,073)
Lower-middle	35.5	50.0	13.0	.8	.7	100	(131,417)
Lower	27.8	62.7	8.3	.3	.8	100	(7,875)
Slum	11.8	84.0	3.0	0.0	1.2	100	(7,875)
Total	40.8	44.6	12.6	1.2	.8	100	(312,427)
	C = .495						
Medellin							
Upper	74.2	7.5	16.5	1.2	.5	100	(9,080)
Middle	57.2	16.5	24.8	.9	.6	100	(20,218)
Lower	23.0	64.5	11.4	.2	.7	100	(55,013)
Total	36.7	46.9	15.2	.4	.7	100	(84,311)
	C = .524						

SOURCE: DANE **Boletin,** No. 229 (August, 1970).

TABLE 29
CLASS VOTING FOR PRESIDENT

	Contingency Coefficient
1968	
Cali, Universidad del Valle survey	.19
1970	
Cali, Universidad del Valle preelectoral survey	.31
Cali, Universidad del Valle postelectoral survey	.47
Bogota, Universidad de los Andes postelectoral survey	.45
Bogota, stratified barrios, official data	.50
Medellin, stratified barrios, official data	.52

Medellin and from the survey in Bogota (Table 28). A more precise way to compare the degree of class voting is to compare the contingency coefficients for the various tables. The contingency coefficient would be zero if all classes voted the same. The figures on Table 29 are adjusted so that the maximum values are one [the C-value $\sqrt{X^2/(N + X^2)}$ is divided by $\sqrt{(K - 1)/K}$]. The contingency coefficient for the 1968 vote is low; it is much higher for all the tables in 1970. The official vote in Bogota proves to have a higher C-value than does the los Andes survey. Class voting in Medellin was even higher, where three-fourths of the upper-class vote went to the official candidate, while two-thirds of the lower-class vote was for Rojas.

Many other factors are related to class voting, and they show the same tendencies but not as strongly. The Anapo vote was strongest among the unskilled workers and the unemployed, and the Pastrana vote was highest among the commercial, managerial, and professional occupations. Education correlates very highly with socioeconomic stratification as well, and gives the same results. The contingency coefficient for education and presidential vote in the preelectoral Valle survey turned out almost identically in Cali with the classification by the socioeconomic level of the barrio.

Whereas it was difficult to get data on socioeconomic stratification outside Cali (we did not want to ask direct questions about income), we do have good information on education. Since results were similar to those for socioeconomic classification in Cali, we can assume there is a similar stratification in the towns and the rural areas as existed in Cali. Table 30 shows that the difference in presidential vote explained by education drops some for towns and even more for rural areas. Nevertheless, one should emphasize the basic similarity rather than the difference. Nearly the same degree of stratification of the vote is reflected in all three areas, and the Rojas campaign was successfully oriented to the common people in all areas, not just the urban ones. Unfortunately it was impossible to conduct a postelectoral survey in the town and rural areas, and we do not know to what extent these areas reflected the strong shift toward greater class voting immediately before and during the elections.

TABLE 30
EDUCATION AND PRESIDENTIAL VOTE

	Contingency Coefficients
Cali	.315
Towns	.297
Rural	.281

TABLE 31
POLITICAL INTEREST AND PRESIDENTIAL VOTE

Interest in Government and Politics	Pastrana Voters	Rojas Voters	Betancur Voters	Sourdis Voters	Nonvoters	Total
Always	20.4	12.9	16.4	0.0	5.8	13.1
Once in a while	50.3	52.7	55.9	68.4	26.4	43.7
Never	29.3	34.4	27.6	31.6	67.8	43.2
Total	100	100	100	100	100	100
n	(622)	(541)	(152)	(19)	(655)	(1,489)

TABLE 32
ATTITUDES ABOUT ELECTIONS (in percentages)

	Yes	No	Don't Know	Total	n
Do you believe that it is important to have elections in our present system?					
Pastrana voters	97.7	.2	2.1	100	(616)
Rojas voters	97.4	1.3	1.3	100	(535)
Betancur voters	98.6	.7	.7	100	(151)
Sourdis voters	88.9	.0	11.1	100	(18)
Nonvoters	83.7	2.8	13.5	100	(600)
Total	93.2	1.4	5.4	100	(1,920)
There is no reason to vote because the individual vote has no importance.					
Pastrana voters	12.1	83.9	4.0	100	(625)
Rojas voters	14.5	80.0	5.5	100	(540)
Betancur voters	11.9	84.2	3.9	100	(151)
Sourdis voters	22.2	77.8	0.0	100	(18)
Nonvoters	31.1	56.7	12.2	100	(656)
Total	19.1	73.7	7.1	100	(1,990)
The vote is a right which should always be exercised.					
Pastrana voters	96.2	2.9	1.0	100	(626)
Rojas voters	96.5	2.4	1.1	100	(539)
Betancur voters	96.1	3.3	.7	100	(153)
Sourdis voters	94.7	5.3	0.0	100	(19)
Nonvoters	70.3	18.8	10.7	100	(660)
Total	87.7	8.1	4.2	100	(1,995)
Democracy does not exist in Colombia because the candidates do not have the same possibilities of being elected.					
Pastrana voters	25.8	64.7	9.6	100	(621)
Rojas voters	57.9	33.3	8.8	100	(539)
Betancur voters	52.6	42.9	4.6	100	(152)
Sourdis voters	63.2	26.3	10.5	100	(19)
Nonvoters	48.8	28.5	22.7	100	(656)
Total	44.5	42.1	13.4	100	(1,987)

OPINIONS OF VOTERS AND NONVOTERS

The previous section showed that the nonvoters and the voters for different candidates had different socioeconomic characteristics. They also have different attitudes and opinions. In fact, these views explain more of the choice to vote or not and for whom than do the socioeconomic characteristics.

The most obvious way in which the voters for all candidates differed from the nonvoters was that they were more interested in politics. Asked whether they were generally interested in governmental and political affairs, about two-thirds of the voters responded either always or once in a while (Table 31). Less than a third of the nonvoters gave similar answers. The Rojas voters are somewhat less interested in politics and government than the voters for the other candidates, but they are much more interested than the nonvoters. The Betancur voters were the most interested.

The voters also tended to give the act of voting and elections more importance than the nonvoters in answering questions that touched upon the vote and the elections (see Table 32). Ninety-three percent of all respondents said elections were important; when asked in a negative way, only 19% agreed that the individual vote was not important. Eighty-eight percent said that one should vote.

On one question—"Democracy does not exist in Colombia because the candidates do not have the same possibilities of being elected, do you agree or disagree?"—however, it was possible to reveal a number of doubts about democracy in Colombia. Almost half the respondents agreed with the statement, and only this last question showed any difference between the voters for different candidates. Fifty-eight percent of the Rojas voters agreed, whereas only 26% of the Pastrana voters did.

Although all voters believed in elections, they differed markedly on their attitudes toward the particular form of democracy which has been instituted in Colombia under the National Front. The question that best showed this difference was the question as to whether it would be best to extend the National Front government, which runs out in 1974. Eight-two percent of the Pastrana voters would like to extend it (Table 33). The Betancur and Sourdis voters were less enthusiastic, but the majority still agreed that it should be extended. On this question, the Rojas voters were even more negative than the nonvoters. The los Andes study in Bogota showed very similar results on the differences between voters when they were asked to evaluate the National Front.

The same conflicting views were also reflected between the voters for

TABLE 33
ATTITUDES ABOUT THE NATIONAL FRONT (in percentages)

	Agree	Disagree	Don't Know	Total	n
The best we could do is to extend the National Front.					
Pastrana voters	82.1	11.7	6.2	100	(625)
Rojas voters	31.3	56.3	12.3	100	(539)
Betancur voters	63.2	28.3	8.5	100	(152)
Sourdis voters	63.2	21.1	15.8	100	(19)
Nonvoters	42.7	30.3	27.0	100	(659)
Total	53.7	31.2	15.1	100	(1,994)

different candidates in their evaluation of the government of the incumbent president, Carlos Lleras Restrepo. This question was asked only on the postelectoral survey, and the response may have reflected the accusations and counteraccusations that accompanied the postelection period. Nevertheless, the support of the Lleras government by the Pastrana voters and the opposition to that government by the Rojas voters shows up very clearly (Table 34). Over 80% of the Pastrana voters considered the Lleras government good or very good. Less than 10% of the Rojas voters thought so. The Rojas voters were a good deal more negative than the nonvoters.

The differences between the opinions of the respondents about less directly political questions may help to explain their attitudes toward the National Front and the Lleras government. Most importantly, the Rojas voters felt that the conditions of life had not improved under the National Front government (see Table 35). Nearly two-thirds of the Rojas voters said it had not improved, as opposed to 12% of the Pastrana voters. Although not very many voters had given the bad economic situation as the reason for voting for their candidate in response to the open question, this great disparity in views must have had a major influence in their

TABLE 34
EVALUATION OF THE GOVERNMENT OF C. LLERAS RESTREPO (postelectoral; in percentages)

	Very Good	Good	Regular (Mediocre)	Bad	Don't Know	Total	n
Pastrana voters	34.9	45.4	15.2	2.1	2.4	100	(335)
Rojas voters	1.6	8.2	50.3	36.7	3.2	100	(316)
Betancur voters	9.7	25.0	50.0	12.5	2.8	100	(72)
Sourdis voters	—	33.3	50.0	16.7	—	100	(6)
Nonvoters	6.2	34.5	35.4	11.4	12.5	100	(455)
Total	13.1	29.5	35.0	15.8	6.6	100	(1,184)

TABLE 35
ECONOMIC CONDITIONS UNDER THE NATIONAL FRONT
(in percentages)

	Yes	No	Don't Know	Total	n
Do you think that living conditions have improved during the National Front?					
Pastrana voters	85.6	11.8	2.6	100	(624)
Rojas voters	30.6	63.6	5.9	100	(542)
Betancur voters	62.6	35.5	2.0	100	(152)
Sourdis voters	52.6	42.1	5.3	100	(19)
Nonvoters	38.4	51.6	9.8	100	(658)
Total	53.0	41.1	5.9	100	(1,995)

decision. Again, the Rojas voters were much more negative than the nonvoters. When asked in the los Andes studies what they considered the most beneficial aspect of their candidate's program, 64% responded in terms of economic aspects.

Despite their negative view about past conditions, the Rojas voters were very hopeful about a future improvement (Table 36). They were one-tenth of a percentage point ahead of the Pastrana voters; they seemed to earnestly believe that Rojas would win and something would be done about their situation. In the preelectoral survey, they also were far more optimistic about the peaceful prospects for the country. (Their feelings after the elections will be discussed later.) Before the election, 56.8% of the Rojas voters disagreed when posed with the proposition that violence would return after the National Front. All groups still were concerned with this problem, but the "don't knows" were large in every group. The

TABLE 36
ATTITUDES ABOUT THE FUTURE (in percentages)

	Yes	No	Don't Know	Total	n
Do you expect an improvement (in living conditions) in the next four years?					
Pastrana voters	91.6	2.7	5.8	100	(625)
Rojas voters	91.7	2.8	5.5	100	(543)
Betancur voters	90.2	3.3	6.5	100	(153)
Sourdis voters	89.5	5.3	5.3	100	(19)
Nonvoters	66.2	16.0	17.8	100	(660)
Total	83.1	7.2	9.7	100	(1,996)
At the end of the National Front, violence will return.					
Pastrana voters	38.8	32.4	28.8	100	(624)
Rojas voters	15.8	56.8	27.4	100	(537)
Betancur voters	21.9	41.0	37.1	100	(151)
Sourdis voters	38.9	27.8	33.3	100	(18)
Nonvoters	23.2	32.1	44.7	100	(655)
Total	26.1	39.5	34.4	100	(1,985)

TABLE 37
DISCONTENT AND VOTING

	Mean Score of Discontent
Pastrana voters	1.87
Rojas voters	4.48
Betancur voters	3.23
Sourdis voters	4.55
Nonvoters	5.34
All	3.91

Rojas voters felt it was less important, which may also help to explain their opposition to the extension of the National Front.

In order to bring together a number of questions that related to the respondents' general feeling about the situation, an index of discontent was built on the basis of answers to eight questions. The questions were weighted toward political matters. Two points were given for a clear statement of discontent and one point for don't know. It can be seen from Table 37 that the Pastrana voters were remarkably content, and only rarely said "don't know." The Rojas voters were not, on the average, as discontent as the nonvoters. The major difference between them came on their views about the electoral process. This index modifies what has been said earlier about motivations to vote or not to vote and for whom. Even though many nonvoters gave their reason for not voting as "lack of interest," they were still on the average more discontent than the voters.

In order to test the relative importance of these different reasons for voting in a way that would make them comparable with the questions asked in the los Andes study, we worked out contingency coefficients for the three most important factors—improvement in living conditions under the National Front; evaluation of the Carlos Lleras government, and the desire to extend the National Front, with the vote for president. Table 38

TABLE 38
IMPORTANCE OF OPINIONS

	Contingency Coefficient
Los Andes Study	
Evaluation of the National Front	.57
Most beneficial aspect of program	.57
Reasons for voting	.53
del Valle Study	
Extend National Front	.54
Evaluation of Lleras government	.71
Conditions of life under National Front	.72

gives these coefficients and compares them with some of the attitudes found in the los Andes study. In the two questions about the living conditions and the evaluation of the Lleras government, we have struck upon very important factors distinguishing the voters for the different candidates, especially the Pastrana and the Rojas voters. The presidential vote is explained better by opinion than by economic position in society, indicating that people who voted for Rojas had more views in common than socioeconomic status. What held them together was the feeling that economic conditions had not improved, that the Lleras government was bad or mediocre, and, to a lesser extent, that the National Front should not be extended.

THE EFFECTS OF THE ELECTION PROCESS

The official returns of the 1970 electon gave the presidency to Misael Pastrana, but the atmosphere that surrounded the counting of the ballots raised doubts about the honesty of the count. Anapo claimed fraud, but the government said the count was honest and countered with the claim that Anapo was trying to foment unrest. What actually happened in the counting of ballots cannot be known with certainty.

Up to 10 p.m. on April 19, the unofficial election results reported by radio and TV showed Rojas winning by a fairly good margin. At 10 p.m., the minister of government announced that there would be no further communication of unofficial results, that the official results would be announced in periodic bulletins. The minister was visibly nervous as he read this announcement on TV. By morning, the official results showed Pastrana winning, and eventually the announcement was made that he had won by a narrow margin. The official explanation was that Rojas did win in the major cities and in many of the larger towns, whose returns came in early, while Pastrana won the smaller towns and districts with less good communications, whose results were reported later.

Rojas and his daughter announced on April 20 that the election results had been falsified, and that they would never accept the legitimacy of Pastrana's government. Shortly after this announcement, riots broke out in all the major cities, and a curfew and martial law were declared. The curfew lasted from 2 p.m. on April 20 until the afternoon of the following day. After that, an 8 p.m. curfew continued in effect for over two weeks, with no sale of liquor allowed. General Rojas and his family were under arrest during this time, and most other important Anapo leaders were also "guarded"—in some cases arrested and later released without formal charges ever having been made. The Anapo newspaper, *Alerta,* was closed for a month.

According to electoral law, the scrutiny of the ballots box by box must be witnessed by a delegate representing each candidate. Anapo at first refused to send delegates, but when the scrutiny continued without them, representatives were sent and ordered to detain the process as much as possible. For two weeks, it seemed that inaugural day (July 20) would come and go without an official final result. However, Anapo did change its tactics and allowed the scrutiny to accelerate. Though still claiming the outcome to be a fraud, Anapo accepted the results of the Congressional Assembly and Council vote, which gave them control (at least 50%) of many councils and assemblies in the country. Through this control, Anapo was able to participate in the patronage hitherto controlled entirely by the traditional parties. Maria Eugenia herself became president of the council of Bogota. In the case of Cali, this tactic was very useful, since the council controlled many of the contracts granted for the Panamerican Games held in Cali in 1971.

When *Alerta* began publishing again after May 20, it continued to report stories about fraud. The clearer statements had to do with pressures applied by governors and local officials. Some Anapo voters claimed they could not vote because their names had been removed from the voters' lists or the polling place had been moved. Though Anapo reporters were not able to find any solid evidence of fraud in the counting of the ballots, they kept repeating the claim.

It will be recalled that the Rojas voters agreed with the voters for the other candidates in the preelectoral survey about the importance of elections, but expressed some doubt about the equality of opportunity for all candidates. The legitimacy of the system of elections seemed high with all groups before the elections. In the survey three weeks after the election, interviewees were asked what they thought about the honesty of the elections and the counting of the ballots. Table 39 shows the answers divided by vote for the presidential candidate. The differences about the freedom and honesty of the elections are not as great as the differences about the honesty of the counting of the ballots. The majority of the sample and a good number of Rojas voters, but not a majority, accepted the honesty of the elections. The Rojas voters, on the other hand, would not accept that the ballots were counted honestly, but held to the view expressed by the Anapo leadership that the election had been stolen from them.

The difference concerning the elections had its impact on other views, and comparing the pre- and postelectoral surveys can get at some of the

TABLE 39
ATTITUDES TOWARD THE ELECTION (in percentages)

	Yes	No	Don't Know
Do you believe that the vote on April 19 was free and honest?			
Pastrana voters	88.4	5.0	,6.6
Rojas voters	41.5	48.4	10.1
Betancur voters	68.1	20.8	11.1
Sourdis voters	83.3	16.7	—
Nonvoters	41.8	22.4	35.8
Total	56.5	24.6	18.9
n = 1,184			
Do you believe that the counting of the ballots was free and honest?			
Pastrana voters	78.5	7.2	14.3
Rojas voters	10.5	77.2	12.3
Betancur voters	38.9	36.1	25.0
Sourdis voters	50.0	50.0	—
Nonvoters	30.8	31.0	38.2
Total	39.0	37.2	23.8
n = 1,184			

impact. It will be recalled that, before the election, the Rojas voters were a very optimistic group. They felt that economic conditions would improve, and they had little fear of a return of violence, about which a question on the postelectoral survey is comparable to the one before the elections. Table 40 gives the responses. Whereas the Pastrana voters expressed some pessimism before the elections, they were more optimistic after the elections. On the other hand, the Rojas voters had decided that there might be some problems of violence after all. As the two questions are not identical, the absolute percentages are not comparable, but the difference between the groups is comparable.

The controversy about the elections also had a serious impact on the legitimacy of the electoral process. Table 41 compares views toward elections among 1968, 1970 preelectoral, and 1970 postelectoral. In 1968,

TABLE 40
VIOLENCE AFTER FOUR YEARS (before and after elections)

	Pastrana	Rojas	Betancur	Sourdis	Nonvoters
Preelectoral					
At end of FN, violence will return—agree	38.7	15.7	21.6	30.8	23.0
Postelection					
After four years there will be more problems of violence	11.6	21.2	16.7	0	20.7
Will be the same	30.5	27.2	34.7	100	27.0

TABLE 41
LEGITIMACY OF ELECTORAL PROCESS
(by class and vote for candidates)

	Class				Weighted Average
	Upper	Middle	Worker	Lower	
1968	89	78	82	79	80
Election important	89	78	82	79	80
1970					
Same question—pre-electoral	99	90	86	91	90
Ought to continue system of elections— postelectoral	82	74	76	72	73

	Voters					
	Pastrana	Rojas	Betancur	Sourdis	Nonvoter	Total
1970						
Election important— preelectoral	96.2	96.1	97.4	84.2	75.8	89.4
Vote is right that should be used— preelectoral	96.2	95.8	95.4	94.7	70.1	87.3
Ought to continue system of elections	86.3	71.8	88.9	66.6	65.6	74.3

there was little interest in the congressional elections in Cali, and the process of elections did not seem as important as it did just previous to the presidential elections in 1970. Three weeks after the election a similar but differently worded question put to the voters showed there was disillusion with the electoral process on the part of followers of both the winners and the losers. The shift was less among the nonvoters, which leads us to believe that the difference in the wording of the questions did not account for the full difference in percentage points. Three-fourths of the population still believed in elections, but the system was shaken by the events surrounding the election.

CONCLUSIONS

The shift from a nonclass, clerical/anti-clerical cleavage to a class-based cleavage in Colombia required that the electorate drop its allegiance to the old parties and then realign its members with parties which represented class divisions. These two steps, although interrrelated, are both histori-cally and behaviorally distinct. The drop in vote for the two traditional parties preceded in time the high vote for Anapo. In addition, many more individuals have ceased to vote for the traditional parties than have decided to vote for Anapo, and others may have voted for Anapo while considering themselves loyal to the traditional parties because nominally the Anapo lists were factions of the traditional parties. Furthermore, as of 1970, it was too early to say that individuals had really committed themselves to a new class party but not too early to say that the loss of commitment to the traditional parties was considerable and increasing.

Although 71% of the electorate was not responding to the organizational call of the parties, the Valle survey indicated that only 26% claimed to be of no party and only 2% mentioned another party, either Anapo, MRL, Communist, or Christian Democrat. In Colombia, party membership is an ascriptive characteristic, and people claim to be a member of a party on the basis of birth, not on the basis of either voting or organizational activity. Therefore, it becomes necessary to interpret from the person's behavior the way he is affiliated with one of the traditional parties. One can say that either voting for Anapo or not voting is a middle step toward becoming totally disaffiliated.

Figure 2 provides a model of how disaffiliation with the traditional party came about. Historically, the process began with the growing intensity of party division in the 1930s and the 1940s, erupting into violence which had three consequences:

(1) it weakened the authority patterns in the rural area;

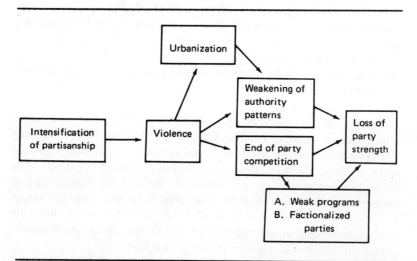

Figure 2: CAUSAL MODEL FOR LOSS OF TRADITIONAL PARTY STRENGTH

(2) it forced internal migration, which also weakened authority patterns; and

(3) the action of political leaders to bring a halt to the violence led first to a nonpartisan military government and then to a coalition government between the parties.

The weakening of the authority patterns led, in turn, to the inability of the gamonales to turn out the vote for the candidates of their choice. The party coalition, with its halting of competition, brought a factionalization of the political parties and a weakening of governmental reform, both of which further reduced party loyalty.

Evidence is not conclusive, but tends to support this model. Table 1 showed that the vote for the traditional party lists has fallen off most in the areas of intense violence. Traditional party vote has also decreased greatly in the cities, but less so in Bogota. That migration to the cities during this period weakened party affiliation is supported by the fact that those who had lived in Cali from five to fifteen years tended to vote less and, when voting, to vote more for Rojas. In the towns and especially in Cali, the adults who have come of voting age during the National Front are much less likely to say that they are members of a party.

Attitudes toward the National Front and Lleras' programs and about living conditions are less closely associated with abstention than with the vote for Rojas, but nevertheless there was a big difference in these attitudes between those who voted for Pastrana and those that either voted for other candidates or did not vote at all. The nonsupporters of Pastrana were far less satisfied with the performance of the National Front and with living conditions. The governmental programs and the living conditions, then, encouraged the loss of support for the traditional parties, but were even more important in determining that the new cleavage would be based on class lines.

Between 1966 and 1970, the Anapo movement more than doubled the percentage of the electorate that voted for it. One-quarter of those interviewed in Valle who indicated they would vote for Anapo said they had never voted before. We do not know how many of the others had not voted in recent elections. However, it is clear that Anapo's support came from the same sectors of the population that had the highest rates of abstention in 1968 and in 1970. They were from the lower classes and were less well educated. Anapo also did somewhat better than the traditional parties among the younger voters and the newer migrants, groups which both had a greater tendency to abstain.

The analysis of the responses to the surveys conducted have identified a number of socioeconomic and opinion variables that related to an individual's choice for president. The use of chi-square and contingency coefficients allowed us to assess the relative strength of these variables, but these nonparametric statistics did not show the interrelations between all of these variables. By reducing the nominal data to a dichotomous form, it is possible to run correlational and path analysis on the data and get some notion of the kind of interrelations. We used only the Rojas and Pastrana voters and only yes and no respondents for the opinion data in order to put these variables into dichotomous form. The length of residence, age, and education were already in a form where meaningful correlations could be run on them. We developed three types of correlation matrices—Pearson's, biserial, and tetrachoric—and then developed path coefficients. The socioeconomic data were put in dichotomous form for the tetrachoric correlations, and the path coefficients for that are shown in Figure 3. The tetrachoric correlation assumes an underlying normality to the distribution that is forced into a dichotomy. The opinion data probably fit this assumption, but the socioeconomic data do not. The coefficients, then, should not be considered to have any precision, but the tendencies indicated in Figure 3 are supported by the other two kinds of correlations, by the contingency tables shown earlier, and by others not reported. We consider Figure 3 an economical way of summarizing relationships that are supported by other kinds of analyses.

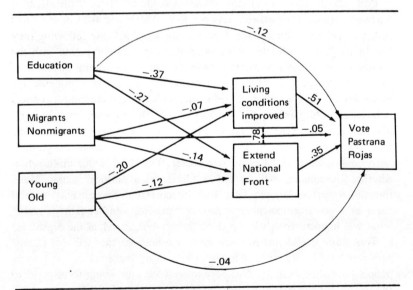

Figure 3: CAUSAL MODEL FOR VOTING CHOICE WITH PATH COEFFICIENTS

The path analyses give us three kinds of new information: first, how much of the relationship between the socioeconomic variables and the vote is direct and how much indirect; second, the relative strength of the different variables; and third, a rough approximation of the total variance in vote that is accounted for by these variables. The relationship of the three socioeconomic variables and the opinion variables are all fairly weak. Education has the strongest relationship and length of residence has the weakest. Most of the influence of these socioeconomic variables on the vote is indirect, through influence on the living conditions and the attitude toward the National Front of the respondents. The direct paths from these two opinions on the vote are quite strong and much stronger than the direct paths of the socioeconomic variables. Responses to these five questions go quite a ways in explaining the way a person will vote. The Pearson's r^2 was .45; the tetrachoric, .76; and the biserial, .84.

Many questions remain unanswered. We have no idea of the depth of the commitment implied by the vote for Rojas to a protest movement or to Anapo in particular. We do not know why the movement that won these votes should be populist and not marxist. We do not know what will happen next. The statistical and historical analyses have, however, clarified some unknowns which will be important in determining the future course of electoral events in Colombia.

Probably the most important unknown is the question of the effect of renewed partisan competition between the Liberals and the Conservatives and, particularly, whether the Liberals can win back the following they had in the late 1940s and 1950s when they stopped competing with the Conservatives. Closely associated with that unknown is the question of what will happen to those who wish to see stronger policies for redistribution. The number of those who wish to see some radical changes is large, especially among the intellectuals. At the moment, they have no place to go. Before the 1970 election, some of them went so far as to say that Anapo was not as bad as the National Front candidates. This group is fairly well divided and has no one leader. The third major unknown is whether Colombians will accept a female as a political leader. Maria Eugenia Rojas de Moreno Diaz has demonstrated the capacity to pull together a good campaign organization, but always in her father's name. What will happen when she has to be the symbol, as well as the organizer?

This study has identified some known conditions that will not change very rapidly. The old partisan loyalties have been weakened and with some people have died entirely. Not very many voters are going to respond to the call of the hereditary hatreds in future elections. Furthermore, a large number of these voters and nonvoters are not satisfied with their present conditions. Only many years of greatly improved economic growth accompanied by some redistribution will satisfy them. In sum, the potential for a radical political movement is here. The only question is whether or not it will be organized by Anapo. Although the vote rose considerably in 1970 over what it had been in the previous election, 54% of the adult population still did not vote. Who will capture their allegiance?

One can imagine three separate possibilities for the future, or some combination of them. If the Liberals fail to regroup and win back their lost following, and the Colombians refuse to accept a female as a political leader, it is most likely that some new radical political movement will arise, perhaps out of the Christian radicals who consider themselves following in the footsteps of Camilo Torres.

If the Liberals can come back with some of the vigor that they had under Gaitan, then they might continue to be the majority force in Colombian politics. In order to win back the masses, they would have to support stronger redistributive measures and develop a capacity to communicate with and organize the masses. Since they still have a large number of wealthy people in their leadership and the local leaders are so concerned with maintaining their positions, it is not certain that the Liberal Party can make these changes.

The last possibility is that the Colombian masses will accept Maria Eugenia as a political leader, and Anapo will remain strong. If so, it could only be defeated by a continued coalition of Liberals and Conservatives. But that coalition seems to be losing support with each passing year, and it has been very weak in picking up young voters. Anapo could, then, quite possibly develop into the majority force.

Most likely is that each of the three unknowns will materialize in some inconclusive way. If so, Colombia would have a very splintered political system, and no power could be concentrated to alleviate the many problems that demand decisive action. More Colombians might then consider the possibility of an end to electoral politics.

EPILOGUE

In the two years that have passed since the April 19, 1970, elections the situation has changed little. The parties have factions similar to those of 1970, and they presented an even greater number of separate lists in the local and departmental elections in 1972 than before. The Pastrana government has made few changes in the programs developed by previous

National Front administrations. In the 1972 elections, the Anapo vote dropped off considerably from what it had been in 1970, though it was still ahead of 1968. Many of the Anapo voters have gone back to abstaining.

The Conservative Party has demonstrated greater unity than it had in recent years as the Ospina wing and the Gomez wing have gone into close cooperation and united their departmental directorates. They have, however, driven off their more progressive wings. Betancur has remained independent and cooperated with Anapo, and J. Emilio Valderrama in Antioquia has gone into opposition since resigning from his position as Minister of Agriculture.

The Liberal Party has manifested a clearer division between its progressive and traditional wings than was the case when Lleras was President. Alfonso Lopez M. and Carlo Lleras, although not particularly active in politics during the period, jointly head the progressive wing. Julio Cesar Turbay heads the more traditional wing. Many of the progressive wing walked out of the 1971 Liberal convention and held their own. The two groups ran different lists in the 1972 elections, and in addition a lot of other factions ran separate lists.

The Pastrana government has had difficulty with Congress because of the large size of the opposition and because the Liberals are concerned with maintaining a separate identity in preparation for the competition against the Conservatives in the 1974 presidential elections. For the most part, Pastrana has maintained administrative continuity with the Lleras administration. The one notable exception came in land reform and agricultural policy. The first appointment as Minister of Agriculture, J. Emilio Valderrama, continued to make moderate progress in the land reform field and in the organization of usuarios. The landowners became increasingly upset and pushed for his resignation, which came after about a year. The new Minister of Agriculture has not aroused the complaints of the landowners, but the Association of Usuarios has become increasingly restive. Where the issue was raised, then, the Pastrana government proved more sensitive to upper-class than to lower-class desires. In the meantime, university students, teachers, and radicals have shown increased discontent, and the government has responded with repression. (Judy Campos has had to finish writing this monograph with the troops outside her window.)

The elections in April 1972 were the first in recent decades that were exclusively for local and departmental representative bodies. Previously, elections for the national Camara were held at the same time. It was predictable, then, that the total vote would go down considerably, and it did sink to the level of the 1968 elections or around 31% by preliminary count. Of these, the Liberal lists received 48%, the Conservative lists, 32% and the Anapo lists 20%.

These local elections indicate that the Liberals, when operating alone, still have considerable strength, and that Anapo still has not welded the kind of commitment that brings out the vote on all occasions. The future strength of Anapo, then, still remains uncertain. In elections at the national level, they could still seriously challenge the traditional parties, but they dropped far enough to make it seem unlikely unless the economic situation deteriorates or the Liberal Party splits.

The lack of commitment of most of the potential electorate remains the most significant development of the National Front period. Nearly 70% of the potential electorate voted for no one. Only 24% of those over 21 voted for either the Liberal or Conservative Parties. A new party or Anapo has a sufficiently large pool of uncommitted to draw upon to take over political power in Colombia.

REFERENCES

ARCINIEGAS, G. (1952) The State of Latin America. New York: Alfred A. Knopf.

BIRD, R. (1970) Taxation and Development. Cambridge, Mass.: Harvard Univ. Press.

COLMENARES, G. (1968) Partidos Politicos y Classes Sociales. Bogota: Edicones Universidad de los Andes.

DIX, R. H. (1967) Colombia: The Political Dimensions of Change. New Haven, Conn.: Yale Univ. Press.

DUFF, E. (1968) Agrarian Reform in Colombia. New York: Frederick A. Praeger.

EDER, R. (1964) "Coup in Colombia hinted by Rojas." New York Times (March 22): 7.

FALS BORDA, O. (1967) La Subversion en Colombia. Bogota: Ediciones Tercer Mundo.

––– (1955) Peasant Society in the Colombian Andes. Gainesville: Univ. of Florida Press.

Flash (1970) "Total oposicion." (June 15): 10-13.

FLUHARTY, V. L. (1957) Dance of the Millions: Military Rule and Social Revolution in Colombia. Pittsburgh: Univ. of Pittsburgh Press.

GIL, F. C. and C. J. PARRISH (1965) The Chilean Presidential Election of September 4, 1964. Washington D.C.: Institute for the Comparative Study of Political Systems.

GINNOLD, R. E. (1971) "The ILO plan for solving the job crisis in Colombia." Monthly Labor Rev. 94: 32-40.

GUZMAN, G. (1968) La Violencia en Colombia. Cali, Colombia: Ediciones Progreso.

HAVENS, A. E. and W. L. FLINN [eds.] (1970) Internal Colonialism and Structural Change in Colombia. New York: Praeger.

HIRSCHMAN, A. (1963) Journeys Toward Progress. New York: Twentieth Century Fund.

Inter-American Development Bank (1970) Socio-economic Progress in Latin America. Washington, D.C.

LLERAS RESTREPO, C. (1966) "La economia de la abundancia frente a la escasez," in Los Caminos del Cambio. Bogota: Ediciones Tercer Mundo.

––– (1963) Hacia la Restauracion Democratica y el Cambio Social. Bogota: Editorial Argra Ltda.

LOTZ, J. R. and E. R. MORSS (1967) "Measuring 'tax effort' in developing countries." International Monetary Fund Staff Papers 14: 478-499.

MARTZ, J. D. (1962) Colombia, a Contemporary Political Survey. Chapel Hill: Univ. of North Carolina Press.

McCAMANT, J. (1971) "Two faces of foreign aid: cooperation and imperialism." (unpublished).

MEACHAM, J. L. (1966) Church and State in Latin America. Chapel Hill: Univ. of North Carolina Press.

MORCILLO, P. P., J. CAMPOS, J. McCAMANT, and H. RIZO (1968) "Estudio sobre abstenticion electoral en las elecciones de Marzo de 1968 en Cali." DANE Boletin Mensual de Estadistica 221.

PAYNE, J. (1968a) "The oligarchy muddle." World Politics 20 (April): 439-453.

––– (1968b) Patterns of Conflict in Colombia. New Haven, Conn.: Yale Univ. Press.

ROJAS DE MORENO DIAZ, M. E. (1970) "Speech delivered in the Plaza Bolivar." Alerta (April 7).

ROSE, R. and D. URWIN (1969) "Social cohesion, political parties and strains in regimes." Comparative Pol. Studies 2 (April): 7-67.

ROWE, J. W. (n.d.) The Argentine Elections of 1963. Washington D.C.: Institute for the Comparative Study of Political Systems.

SANTA, E. (1964) Sociologia Politica de Colombia. Bogota: Ediciones Tercer Mundo.

SMITH, T. L. (1967) Colombia, Social Structure and the Process of Development. Gainesville: Univ. of Florida Press.

TAYLOR, M. C. (1965) Fiscal Survey of Colombia. Baltimore: John Hopkins Press.

TORRES, C. (1970) "Social change and rural violence in Colombia," in I. L. Horowitz (ed.) Masses in Latin America. New York: Oxford Univ. Press.

United Nations Food and Agricultural Organization (1971) "Colombia—reforma agraria e instituciones, resultados politicos." DANE Boletin Mensual de Estadistica 242: 145-160.

U.S. Senate Committee on Foreign Relations (1969) Survey of the Alliance for Progress, Colombia a Case History of U.S. Aid. Washington D.C.: U.S. Government Printing Office.

Universidad de los Andes (1970) "El voto presidencial en Bogota. Analisis de comportamiento electoral del 19 de Abril de 1970." DANE Boletin Mensual de Estadistica 224 (August).

VERGARA DELGADO, H. (1970) "Speech delivered in Bogota." Alerta (April 10).

VILLAVECES, J. [ed.] (1968) Los Mejores Discursos de Jorge Eliecer Gaitan. Bogota: Editorial Jorir.

APPENDIX: SURVEY PROCEDURES

In 1970, two members of the Department of Social Sciences of the Universidad del Valle made a survey research study on the elections of April 19, 1970. The first survey was made from March 10 to April 17, with questionnaires, administered in six municipios: Cali, La Cumbre, El Cerrito, Roldanillo, Puerto Tejada, and Padilla. In Cali, approximately 1,200 interviews were made: 6.7% upper class, 11.7% middle class, 30.8% working class, and 50.8% lower class. The distribution was based on January 1969 data from the Cali Municipal Planning Office.

The sample was selected in the following manner: the classification of barrios of the Municipal Planning Office was used and then complemented by an independent classification made by impartial judges who knew Cali. They reconciled both classifications of barrios and divided them into the four socioeconomic groups. The limitation of this process is recognized, as there are many barrios in which residents are of various socioeconomic levels. With a list of all barrios of Cali divided into four socioeconomic groups, random selection of the barrios which would be objects of study proceeded.

The total number of interviews which would be made in each socioeconomic subgroup was randomly determined by mathematical methods with regard to considerations of time and cost. Once these barrios were selected, the homes in which the interviews would be done were chosen, again by random means. Each interviewer was told in which house to conduct his first interview, he was instructed then to go to every fourth house along a barrio street. In each barrio, the first house was randomly selected and therefore selection of every fourth house was also random.

The questionnaire, designed by the professors of the Department of Social Sciences (Professors Campos, Hammock, and Rivas) and the students of the Social Research Seminar, could be administered in 20 minutes.

The interviews in Cali were made from April 8 to 17, the great majority being made on April 11 and 12, one week before the election. The interviewers were all students at the Universidad del Valle. Of the 45 total interviewers used, 10 were members of the Seminar on Social Research Methods of the Department of Social Sciences. These students performed as team leaders, supervising the interviewing students.

The methodology used in the municipios was different and probably less scientific. However, the scientist encounters a series of grave problems in making interviews in small, very rural municipios. It was attempted to make a study of the entire municipio and not only the cabecera. This involved problems of transportation to out-of-the-way veredas. But even in the cabecera one cannot use the stratification classification used in Cali, since there is much less reliability in making classification of socioeconomic groups by barrios in the towns. Furthermore, a simple random sample is impossible because complete lists of the total population do not exist.

The procedure was as follows: the percentage of the population of a municipio living in the cabecera was determined using 1964 census data. Then it was determined how many lived in each town and each vereda. For La Cumbre and El Cerrito, the data were more complete, due to the existence of a study of the Centro Universitario de Investigacion sobre Poblacion (CUIP), which had made a complete census of the area. The approximate number of total interviews needed for each municipio was estimated. The percentage of interviews in each cabecera was assigned corresponding to its proportion of the municipios total population. For example, in the municipio of El Cerrito, 60% of the municipio's interviews were needed in the town of Cerrito. In La Cumbre, only 35% were made in the cabecera. Within the cabecera, the following procedure was followed: the interviewers all started from the center of the town, and interviewers were assigned to work out from there to different sectors of the town. Interviews were conducted in every fourth house, and in El Cerrito and La Cumbre, almost every street of the town was reached. In Puerto Tejada and Roldanillo, where less information about the town was available, and the population was greater, only a few interviewers reached the periphery, where the poorest people in both towns live. Thus, in both towns, the sample is not as representative as would have been desired. In both municipios, the interviews were made in one day.

The sample of the rural part of the municipios was chosen randomly in El Cerrito and La Cumbre. Since there existed census data of all the veredas of the municipio, the veredas were placed on a list and chosen randomly, to the extent that the total number of interviews necessary was approached. Thus, in Cerrito, the following veredas were included: Santa Elena, Tenerife, El Paraiso, Carrizal, and San Antonio.

In La Cumbre, the same method was used, although it had to be modified a little because of the problems of transportation in that municipio (few roads suitable for motor vehicles.) Interviews were conducted in: La Cumbre, Lomitas, Pavas, and Puente Palo.

In Roldanillo, included were Tierra Blanca, Higueroncito, Morcha (Higueron), and la Seca.

In Puerto Tejada, included were: Puerto Tejada, Ortigal, and some interviewers went as far as Padilla, all relatively near the cabecera. For lack of time, towns more remote could not be reached. The rural areas where interviews were conducted were chosen by coincidence, without any random sampling.

The following numbers of interviews were conducted: Cali—1,220; El Cerrito—267; La Cumbre—226; Puerto Tejada and Padilla—221; Roldanillo—234.

In all the towns surveyed, the people appeared interested. In the municipios outside Cali, there were very few refusals of the questionnaire, although the campesino often had to be convinced that his opinion, and not only that of the leaders, was wanted. In the rural areas, responses of "don't know" were fairly common.

In Cali, there were some refusals in the lower and working classes. The number of refusals in the lower classes was 51; in the working class, 29; in the middle class, 8; and in the upper class 0; total number of refusals—88. The reasons for the refusals varied from "I don't have time," to "this is purely political," and "this must be for a candidate." The number of refusals was not so high (5%) as to cast doubt upon the validity of the sample, given its size. Although there were refusals, there was only one incident, when a student tried to interview a man who was under the influence of alcohol.

THE SECOND ELECTORAL STUDY

A postelectoral study was planned for the week following the election. As a consequence of the political situation of the week of the 26th (state of siege declared following riots in major cities), it was not possible to make the study until three weeks later. The study was done solely in Cali. Although it was planned to return to the same houses in which the first interviews had been made, it was decided because of the political situation to go to different houses. The same barrios, but different houses, were selected. Some 1,200 interviews were made.

The questionnaire, much shorter than the first, could be administered in ten to fifteen minutes. There were no problems and an insignificant number of rejections.

COMPARISON OF THE SAMPLE AND THE OFFICIAL ELECTORAL RESULTS

The comparison of the official data with our sample shows two points which need to be discussed. First, there was a fairly large discrepancy between the proportion of our interviewees who said they would vote or had voted and the actual proportion that did vote. In the interviews, 66% of the preelectoral sample for all of Valle claimed they would vote, and 62% of the postelectoral Cali respondents said they did. According to official figures presented by DANE, 45.6% of the population over 21 of Valle voted in the April 19, 1970, election, and 38.3% of the population over 21 in Cali voted.

Second, according to the sample, Pastrana had more voters than Rojas (Pastrana–42.1%; Rojas–36.8%) whereas the official results show Rojas winning in Valle: Rojas–48.0% and Pastrana–38.9%. There is a much smaller difference in the figures for Betancur (sample: 1.6%; official: 1.03%).

JUDITH TALBOT CAMPOS is currently Assistant Professor of Political Science in the Division of Social and Economic Sciences of the Universidad del Valle, Cali, Colombia. She received her B.A. from Grinnell College and her M.A. from the University of Wisconsin. She has coauthored two articles on elections in Colombia published in the D.A.N.E. Boletin Mensual de Estadistica. *Her fields of interest include comparative and Latin America politics and political parties.*

JOHN F. McCAMANT is currently Associate Professor in the Graduate School of International Studies, University of Denver. He served for two years (1966-1968) as Visiting Professor at the Universidad del Valle under the Rockefeller Foundation University Development Program. He received his B.A. from Carleton College, his M.A. from Columbia University, and his Ph.D. from the University of Washington. He is author of Development Assistance in Central America *(Praeger, 1968) and several articles published in professional journals. His fields of interest include social cohesion and political economy.*

DATE DUE